Haunted
Places
of
Sussex

Judy Middleton

COUNTRYSIDE BOOKS
NEWBURY BERKSHIRE

First published 2005
© Judy Middleton 2005

COUNTRYSIDE BOOKS
3 Catherine Road
Newbury, Berkshire

To view our complete range of books,
please visit us at
www.countrysidebooks.co.uk

ISBN 1 85306 920 5
EAN 978 1 85306 920 8

Cover picture from an original
by Anthony Wallis

Designed by Peter Davies, Nautilus Design
Produced through MRM Associates Ltd., Reading
Printed by Arrowsmith, Bristol

• Contents •

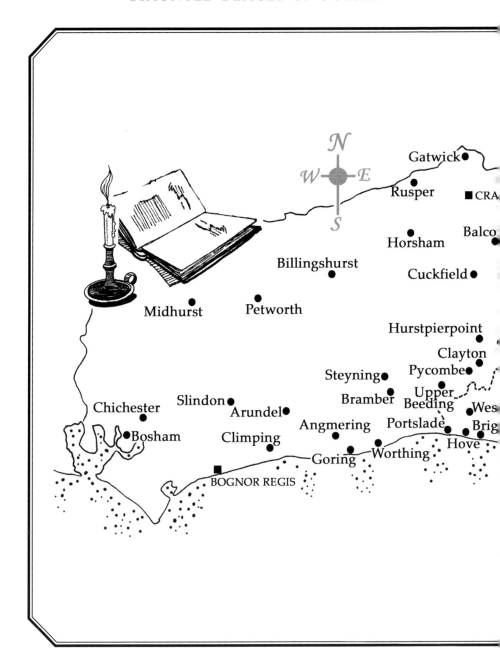

EAST GRINSTEAD

Crowborough

ywards Heath

Buxted

Burwash

Bodiam

vesfield

ss Hill

ng

eston

Rye

BATTLE

Winchelsea

Herstmonceux

Lewes

gton

Hailsham

Hastings

Alfriston

Westham

Bexhill

ean

Jevington

Eastbourne

Seaford

· Introduction ·

Ghost stories are as old as mankind and yet interest in them has never been greater than it is today. People who see a ghost do not all have the same reaction. Some refuse to discuss the experience; others will relate the story but do not want to be identified, while a few are happy to tell you about it and do not object to their name being mentioned. Although ghost-hunting can be a fascinating business, it can also be frustrating when promising leads peter out because someone refuses to speak to you.

People seeing a ghost unexpectedly are often intrigued more than anything else. But for a few, it can be a shocking experience. Many ghosts are simply poor souls who have lost their way towards the afterlife and for one reason or another stay trapped on earth. All they need is a gentle, prayerful prod to set them off gratefully in the right direction.

But there are other more malevolent spirits abroad and these must be treated with caution. And, while on this subject, I feel it would be wise to stress the importance of not getting involved with an ouija board. If your house is haunted, and it scares you, your first line of approach should be to your local parish priest who will put you in touch with one who specialises in exorcism.

In this book you will find a variety of stories from this much-haunted corner of England. A few are part and parcel of Sussex lore but there are some new accounts to intrigue the reader.

Judy Middleton

• West Sussex •

ANGMERING

There is a local tradition of a monk of enormous size in the vicinity of Ecclesden Manor, a long flint-built house that was erected in 1634. Some people think the site was formerly occupied by a monastic structure. If so it would not be surprising as there were other religious houses in the area, with the Knights Hospitallers at Poling and Benedictine nuns at Lyminster, both to the west of Angmering. Perhaps Ecclesden's spectre suffered eviction, along with his fellow monks, at the time of the Dissolution of the Monasteries from 1536 onwards.

One recorded sighting was in late August 1964, at around 7 pm, when Roy Chambers, a farm worker, was opening a gate to a field that was situated between Highdown Hill and Ecclesden Manor. He noticed a monk dressed in a brown habit sitting on a bank reading a prayer book. At first there seemed nothing at all out of the ordinary about the figure. But when the monk suddenly stood up, it was apparent he must be between 8 and 9 feet tall. By this time Chambers was a mere three yards from the apparition and he was so unnerved that he moved away as quickly as he could. When he took a quick glance over his shoulder there was no sign of the monk.

* * *

Parts of the Lamb Inn, which looks out over The Square, date back to the 16th century and it was extended in the early 18th century. As it was a coaching inn serving the old route from London to Littlehampton, there were large stables at the back reached through the arch that can still be seen on the west side. Legend has it that the room near the

The Lamb Inn, Angmering.

archway once served as a mortuary – perhaps the notion arose out of the former practice of holding inquests in pubs as they were often the only buildings large enough and locally situated in which a coroner's court could be conducted. This area was subsequently used as a bottle store but the bedroom above is said to be haunted by a Woman in White. Another ghost has been seen by several people in the inn itself – a man dressed in Victorian clothes warming himself by sitting on the stool by the fireplace, which has a 17th century fireback featuring the royal coat-of-arms. In addition, in 1991 landlord Russell Hall said that footsteps were often heard when there were no guests in the house.

ARUNDEL

The ancient parish church of Arundel enjoys the unique distinction of encompassing two separate denominations – Roman Catholic and the Church of England. This is because the eastern part (the Fitzalan Chapel) and the Lady Chapel to the north originally formed the private chapel of the College of Holy Trinity (Arundel Priory), which, in 1544, Henry VIII sold for 1,000 marks to Henry, 12th Earl of Arundel. Thus the Fitzalan Chapel continued to be used as the family mortuary chapel. The rest of the edifice became an Anglican church dedicated to St Nicholas.

During the Civil War the Roundheads occupied the building as a barracks while their horses were stabled amongst the alabaster and marble likenesses of successive earls and dukes in the Fitzalan Chapel. The soldiers gave vent to their Puritan beliefs by smashing every bit of stained glass as well as mutilating frescos and effigies. The peaceful atmosphere of the chapel was thus rudely violated. Might this account for the sense of antagonism and icy chill perceived by some visitors? Perhaps it is the frustrated energy of aristocrats whose last resting place has been so cruelly shattered.

The church of St Nicholas, Arundel.

In 1983, for example, a family, Mr and Mrs Wilkinson and their children, visited the chapel and while the youngsters preferred to remain outside and amuse themselves by rolling down the grassy bank, their parents stepped inside to look around. Mrs Wilkinson immediately felt an empathy with one of the female effigies, but her husband was so disturbed by the unwelcoming atmosphere that he hurried back outside, muttering that he could not stay. Quite independently, two friends of the family visited the chapel a couple of years later and, without knowing of their experiences, reported feelings of cold hostility.

Bernard Marmaduke of Arundel Castle, 16th Duke of Norfolk, Earl Marshal and Premier Earl of England, died on 31st January 1975. Not long after the funeral Howard Frith, a churchwarden, happened to look into the chapel from the St Nicholas side and noticed what he assumed to be a white-haired family mourner kneeling before the altar. The figure was clad in a long blue robe. It was not until he mentioned it to the gardener that he realised he must have seen a ghost because the gardener said the chapel was locked up and he had the key. When they went to check, the chapel door was still locked and there was nobody inside.

BALCOMBE

On 17th June 1839 an inquest was held at the Half Moon pub. It concerned the fate of navvy William Hanbury, who had been employed on railway construction nearby. He and his mates were excavating a bank when part of it collapsed on top of him. But it does not seem as though the two ghosts at the pub have any connection with him. One is the usual sort of cellar ghost who likes to move objects around, and the other is sometimes heard singing in the yard behind.

However, there are ghosts connected with the Balcombe railway tunnel that do not belong to erstwhile construction workers. It seems that during the First World War three soldiers taking part in an exercise decided to seek shelter from the rain inside the tunnel. It was a foolhardy decision because a train killed them. Three ghosts have since been seen, always together, looking real enough in their old-style uniforms but then quickly fading away. One sighting occurred in the Second World War when a patrolling soldier spotted them and again in 1995 some youngsters saw them. The fact that three soldiers were killed in the tunnel has an eerie modern parallel because three Territorial Army soldiers were killed in recent times in Clayton Tunnel, to the south (see Clayton).

In the Victorian era a curate who was living in lodgings in Balcombe was conducting a restrained courtship of a well-educated young lady. They would often take long walks together. On one occasion, deep in conversation, they turned into a field and walked along a hedgerow only to be brought abruptly to a horrifying halt. There in front of them, dangling from the end of a rough cart rope, was the dead body of a labourer. When they had recovered somewhat from their fright, they decided that their best course of action was to fetch the local constable. As they left the scene, they glanced back at the fatal tree and were astonished to see no sign of the hanged man. It later transpired that several villagers had also seen the hanging ghost and the story was that a local man had committed suicide at the spot. But what is even more curious was that the manifestation also included a branch of the tree that was no longer in existence as the offending branch had been struck by lightning some time after the deed.

BILLINGSHURST

The King's Arms is an old coaching inn and so it is appropriate that a coachman should haunt it. The story goes that one night in February this coachman had imbibed rather too much good ale and he was unsteady on his feet when he went to make a final check on the horses before

The King's Arms, Billinghurst in the 1920s. (Picture courtesy of Robert Jeeves)

turning in. He stumbled across the yard, missed his footing and fell down the well. It is said the well was exceptionally deep and his body was never recovered. Let us hope there was an alternative water supply.

BOSHAM

E dward Bennett was an irascible old man. In spite of living in such beautiful and tranquil surroundings he was usually so bad tempered that the villagers learned to leave him alone. He also vented his ill humour on his son and they had a bitter quarrel. It was a pity because his son was a sailor and so his visits were infrequent anyhow. After the final quarrel the sailor stopped making his way to Bosham to see his father when his ship docked in home waters. On his deathbed Edward Bennett bitterly regretted his behaviour and his ghost is said to haunt Bosham Manor House. His mournful face gazes out at the creek, waiting for a sight of his son.

A lovely old postcard view of Bosham.

BRAMBER

Wartilliam the Conqueror granted no less than 38 Sussex manors to William de Braose, besides large estates in Wales, Dorset and Hampshire. The principal seat of the de Braoses in Sussex was Bramber Castle and the family became so rich and powerful that in later years King John considered them to be a threat. His wrath fell on William de Braose, great-grandson of the William previously mentioned. Young William had married Matilda de St Viliare and there were five children – the heir Reginald, who was considerably older than the rest of his siblings, William, Blanche, Jane and the infant Hugh. Reginald went to live in a castle in Ireland.

In 1208 King John sent a messenger to Bramber Castle. The dreadful message he bore was that the King wanted the de Braose children as hostages to guarantee their father's loyalty to the crown. Matilda was a spirited lady and it was she who spoke out and said she could not possibly entrust her children to a monarch who had apparently murdered his nephew, Prince Arthur, whom he was honour-bound to pro-tect. The messenger returned to the King empty-handed, leaving conster-nation behind. As the de Braoses knew that Bramber Castle was in no position to withstand a siege they had no option but to flee to Ireland. Although they made a safe landing, there was treachery afoot, which resulted in Matilda and her children being captured and taken to London. From there they were conveyed by covered barge to Windsor Castle where they were thrown into the dungeons and slowly starved to death. Meanwhile, William de Braose and Reginald managed to escape to France but William soon died of a broken heart. The gaunt ghosts of the de Braose children were said to haunt the main street of Bramber at Christmas time, begging for bread.

The impressive remains of the gate tower at Bramber Castle, 1908.

CHICHESTER

By the 2nd century AD a wall had been built to safeguard Chichester – known as Noviomagus during the Roman occupation – and number 38 West Street, now a pub, is built almost hard up against its west side. If you open the side door at the back you are confronted with a tall flint-built wall immediately in front of you. During the Civil War the building on the site was used as a guardhouse when there was a garrison in Chichester. But there has been a public house there since the 1750s – at first it was called the Three Kings and subsequently the Duke of Richmond. It was known as the Castle from the 1790s to the 1990s but since 1992 it has had its present name, the Chichester.

It has long been claimed that the ghost of a Roman centurion still patrols the old walls and that his passage takes him straight through the pub. If the ghost does date from Roman times it seems more likely that he was a legionary, since a centurion was a senior soldier, a com-mander – but people have always called him a centurion and so it is pointless to

Shirley Brennan behind the bar of the Chichester pub in West Street, Chichester.

quibble. The patrolling spectre has been seen by many people while others have felt him brush past. The whole figure is not in view, just the top half. This could be explained by different ground levels since Roman times. Chichester would not be unique in still being frequented by a Roman soldier, as there was a famous case in York where several Roman legionaries were seen, led by another on horseback.

On 25th February 2004 thirteen ghost hunters spent the night in the Chichester pub. They belonged to a Bognor-based group called SPIRIT (Sussex Paranormal Research and Investigation Team) and the event was also a fund-raising effort for 4Sight – a Sussex charity that helps the blind. The participants arrived with high expectations and bearing ghost-detecting equipment such as night-vision digi-cams, EMF (electro magnetic field) meters and infrared thermometers. A Roman coin, a ring and a brooch were placed near the centurion's beat to act as trigger objects, and the group held hands in a circle and were asked to meditate and visualise colours to make them more receptive.

After midnight a sudden drop in temperature was recorded as lasting for five minutes. Andrew Gadd, a psychic medium, explained that the centurion had passed through but he was not expected to return for some 50 minutes or so. The equipment recorded further activity at 2 am, 3 am and 4 am. The volunteers saw nothing but later on when the film footage was examined some 'interesting light anomalies' were visible. These anomalies coincided with the camera's power deceasing and the EMF meter going off.

In old premises such as these it often happens that the presence of one spirit seems to attract others – perhaps the original one acts as a sort of gateway. In February 2004 Shirley Brennan and Nick Webb became landlords of the Chichester, having moved from Aylesbury in Buckinghamshire. A barmaid told them that one day in the previous month she had been busy polishing the large mirror that hung opposite an entrance when she spotted the figure of an old woman in the doorway. On turning around to inform the potential customer the pub was not yet open, she found there was nobody there.

Shirley and Nick soon became aware of cold spots on the premises, and door latches lifting up on their own. But what angered Shirley was being continually woken up in the night at 4.23 am precisely. She did not see a ghost but at length she became so exasperated that she shouted out, 'If you don't stop waking me up, I'll call the exorcist in.' Apparently, the spirit paid heed and she has not been troubled since.

* * *

Unicorn House, Eastgate, Chichester.

Unicorn House is situated in Eastgate at the end of East Street. It was built on an ancient site that once served as a Roman cemetery where cremated remains were placed in burial urns, and East Street was once part of the famous Stane Street – the cross-country link with London. By mediaeval times there was a victualling house there, which in 1670 was replaced by the Unicorn Inn. It soon became associated with a brewery and was rebuilt around 1760. The inn was still in use in the 20th century and there was a dance hall upstairs. During the Second World War this was frequented by airmen from RAF Tangmere, where three Hurricane squadrons were based in 1940. The Unicorn ceased trading in 1960 and the present-day building houses the offices of the *Chichester Observer*.

This brief outline gives some idea of the continuous use of the site, built over years like layers of a cake. In a similar way, the spirits in the building do not come from one era. Although there have been no Roman sightings, the negative energy detected by one medium might emanate from the site's use as a cemetery. In 2004 another medium visited Unicorn House and found it 'teeming with spirits'. Surely the most poignant ghost she encountered was the boy from Victorian times sobbing under the stairs. She discovered that he had become separated from his mother after a fire. But the story has a happy ending as the medium managed to locate his mother, who came back to fetch her child. The medium also spotted an army general comfortably ensconced in the corner of the editor's office. He was described as a friendly old gentleman who just sat there watching the editor at work. Not quite so pleasant was a discontented spirit located in the photographic area, apparently pacing up and down, sapping energy. No doubt this entity was behind a recent incident when a heavy office guillotine, securely in place, was flung off the top of a cabinet. When paranormal investigators came to Unicorn House quite recently they filmed the photographic area and the developed film showed orbs of light flitting about, which was explained as a visible sign of the spirits' energy.

However, no medium has come across any airmen so far – although it has long been believed that a pilot, from the Second World War likes to revisit the happy times he spent in the dance hall.

In the summer of 2004, while alone in the building, the night cleaner saw a male figure at the top of the stairs. It is amusing to note that the ghosts keep up with the latest technology and sometimes keyboard keys have been pressed when nobody was using them. But the spirits still perform old-fashioned tricks such as slamming doors and pulling drawers in and out.

CLAYTON

It would not be an exaggeration to call the little house that nestles between two Gothic-inspired towers at the north entrance to Clayton Tunnel on the Brighton to London railway line the most unusual dwelling in Sussex. The first remark people usually make is that it must be frightfully noisy. Surprisingly the answer is no. The noise of the train is pushed into the tunnel and only a slight vibration reaches the house above. Nor does the house become enveloped in clouds of smoke and smuts as it must have done in the days before electrification.

The story is that when the land was sold to the railway company, the landowner stipulated the tunnel entrance must be made distinctive and not be merely a black hole in the hillside – hence the Gothic folly. Tunnel House was built in the 1830s and served as a wages office for workers toiling on the railway cutting. After that it became a glorified mess room where gangers brewed up in their break time. Lastly it became a dwelling house and although only tiny with just two bedrooms, it seemed to attract large families. Mr Russell, head ganger, and his wife brought up a family of nine

The little house between the towers of Clayton Tunnel entrance.

children, and the third occupants, the Attmeres, had six children. The latter came to live there in 1956, renting it from British Rail.

Mrs Muriel Attmere, later Mrs Greenwood, loved living there because it was so peaceful and rural – in spite of the place being haunted. She said the ghosts were not frightening or she would not have remained for nigh on 38 years. One ghost was nicknamed Charlie although nobody knew his real identity. In one of the towers there is a sealed-off entrance to an inspection tunnel leading to ventilation shafts. It was in this inspection tunnel that footsteps were heard as well as eerie noises like screams or sighs. People have thought that, because of the location, it might be the ghost of an old ganger. When the entrance was doubly sealed Muriel often found herself thinking, 'Poor old Charlie, now he's stuck there.'

The sceptics would say the sounds were nothing more than the wind playing tricks in the tunnels but that does not explain noises Muriel heard inside her home. She was sometimes aware of a drumming sound on the table in her living room, just as though some man were sitting there, tapping his fingers impatiently.

Then there was the glow spotted on one of the towers, which Muriel saw more than once. It was not a will o' the wisp light, but the outline of a man of medium height, seen both at dusk and later at night. Although the sounds did not disturb her, the glow certainly did. When she saw it she would never investigate but would turn round smartly and go back indoors.

There was also a White Lady. Although Muriel could sense her presence at times, she never saw the ghost. But two of her grandchildren (she had eleven) certainly did and called her to their bedroom to make it go away.

In part of Muriel's garden there was an orchard of apple, pear and plum trees. Although it was a lovely place, she did not care to linger there after dark because it had a powerfully sad atmosphere. This was not surprising when you realise that corpses of people who had met an untimely end in Clayton Tunnel were formerly brought out and laid on this stretch of grass. Indeed it was a marvel that Tunnel House should have turned out to be such a happy home when so many tragedies have occurred close by.

The most horrific accident happened on a Sunday morning in August 1861. The railway line had been operating for twenty years and the holiday season was in full swing. There was supposed to be a safe interval between train departures but survivors claimed three trains left Brighton Station at 8.28, 8.31 and 8.35 am. Signalman Killick was on duty at Clayton Tunnel. He had no assistant and worked for 24 hours at a stretch every other Sunday for a wage of £1 a week.

What happened was that the first train was delayed in the tunnel and so Killick waved his red flag to stop the second train – the mechanical signal having failed. The driver of the second train saw the red flag but could not make a dead stop and the train ran into the tunnel for a considerable distance. Once it had stopped, the driver began slowly to reverse it out. Meanwhile, the third train was fast approaching and Killick, having heard a train leave the tunnel (he thought it was the second one but in fact it was the first one) gave the all clear. The third train then entered the tunnel and although the unfortunate driver spotted the tail-lights of the second train, he was unable to prevent his engine from steaming right over the rear carriages. A scene of utter confusion ensued, made worse by the pitch darkness. The tunnel was completely blocked by the debris of engine and splintered carriages, and the tender continued to vent steam and boiling water over the dead and injured passengers. As well as 176 injured passengers, at least 23 people were killed, including three children, and a couple of bodies were never identified. One can imagine the terrified screams and it is perhaps not surprising that echoes could still be heard in later years.

There was another accident in the tunnel in 1926, and in 1973 three Territorial Army soldiers were killed there while taking part in a map reading exercise. Muriel gave evidence at the inquest.

In 1994 Muriel was devastated to have to leave her unique home because of ill health. She moved to a modern flat in Burgess Hill and died less than a month later.

* * *

Clayton Manor, which was erected in 1720 and extended in 1750 and 1850, stands in Underhill Lane – a descriptive name for a road that literally runs along the foot of the Downs. The ancients favoured this sheltered place and there was once a Roman villa close by. Later a monastery was built on the site. There are at least three ghosts that haunt the house – a Roman centurion whose grave was disturbed in the 1920s, a monk who is apt to appear in the dining room, and a crying baby.

A famous recent resident was the horror writer Peter James who was born at Hove in 1948. His mother Cornelia was a glove maker to royalty. His father always wanted to be a writer and James said he could sense his presence strongly when he began to write his first book. James is an ideal occupant for a haunted house as he is interested in the occult and benefited from the advice of the Revd Canon Dominic Walker, the Church of England's expert on the subject, and now Bishop of Monmouth. One of James's most memorable books is *Prophecy*, which is based on a real-life experience when a group of friends held a session with an ouija board whose disturbing answers to questions all came true.

CLIMPING

In the village of Climping there is a venerable house now known as Brookpits Manor, a sturdily built yeoman's dwelling dating back to the early 17th century. It boasts original mullioned windows and was constructed of flint with brick dressings – an early example of this style. In the 20th century Lord Moyne owned the property and he used it to house workers from his estate or aged retainers.

Mr E. Wingate was an estate worker who lived there in the 1920s and he regularly got up at 4.30 am to see to the farm stock. On one particular morning he came downstairs as usual but as he entered the living room he noticed a figure sitting quietly in an old high-backed chair. The ghost did not vanish as soon as it was seen and so Wingate had a good opportunity to notice all the details. In front of him was a large, thickset man with heavy features and a full, light-coloured beard. He was dressed in dark clothes covered with a cape and on his head he sported one of those old-fashioned tall silk hats popularly called stovepipes. It seemed as though he were waiting patiently for something – perhaps for his carriage to roll up to the door. But as the ghost sat there with his hands resting lightly on the arms of the chair, he gradually faded away. Soon Wingate found himself gazing at an empty chair.

At work later that day Wingate told his fellow workers about his ghostly visitor. Not surprisingly most of them thought he was spinning a yarn and they did not take him seriously. But one friend believed the story and told him of an infallible method of ensuring that the ghost did not keep returning. Wingate was instructed to cut a bramble, taking care it was a thick, green specimen, and to carry it upstairs with him when he retired for the night.

Next morning Wingate made his way downstairs armed with the bramble and there was the ghost sitting in the chair. Acting upon his friend's instructions, Wingate quietly lifted the bramble branch and made a sawing motion to and fro on the edge of the door. There was no gentle fading away this time but an abrupt disappearance. Moreover the ghost was never seen again.

The use of a bramble to exorcise the ghost is a most unusual aspect of this story. Wherever did Wingate's friend learn of this trick? Folklore connected with the humble bramble suggest that if it blossoms near the beginning of June, there will be an early harvest; if the leaves are dark and spotted, that is a sign of sickness in the area. An arch of bramble firmly rooted at both ends was considered to be powerful magic and children suffering from whooping cough were drawn through it backwards. It was also efficacious for children afflicted with boils, and cattle were driven through such an arch to act as a general insurance policy.

In 1972 Mr V. Landymore purchased Brookpits Manor from Lord Moyne's daughter. There followed two years of extensive restoration. During the course of the work, several of the men employed there told Mr Landymore about a female ghost seen coming through a downstairs window on several occasions. Oddly enough she was entering the same room in which the ghost with the stovepipe hat had been seen. However, that window was blocked up and two rooms were knocked into one to create more space. The female ghost seemed to withdraw too and has not been seen since. The house is quiet – that is as peaceful as you would expect an old house to be. There are creaks and bumps as old timbers settle and the vibrations of somebody moving around in one part of the house can be transmitted via the beams to another part. You can never be quite sure whether you are hearing a normal sound or if things still go bump in the night.

CUCKFIELD

Ockenden House (later known as Ockenden Manor) has an old timber-framed part on the north side to which a new wing built of stone was added in 1608. There are underground passages and a secret hiding place for a priest dating from the time when it was extremely hazardous being a Roman Catholic.

For many years Ockenden House was the seat of the Burrell family. Sussex diarist Timothy Burrell was born at Cuckfield in 1643 and forty years later inherited the house. He was a compassionate man and in October 1709 when

The north-facing front of Ockenden Manor.

there was 'a dearth of provisions' he resolved to give food to any poor person who might arrive at his door on a Sunday and ask for it. Over the winter months he was prepared to give out between 12 lbs and 16 lbs of beef weekly, and a bushel of wheat and a half-bushel of barley spread over four weeks.

The Raymond Room, Ockenden Manor.

Ockenden Manor is now a hotel with 22 bedrooms. Joan Forman, who published *The Haunted South* in 1978, first heard about the Grey Lady reputed to haunt the house several years before she actually stayed there. When she did spend the night she slept peacefully and saw no sign of the ghost. The oak-panelled haunted chamber was called the Raymond Room. One honeymoon couple found it too eerie for their taste and the bride positively refused to stay there. Another guest, this time an elderly lady, slept in the Raymond Room but once was quite enough and she requested the manager never to allocate that room to her again. Unfortunately, none of the people would give any indication of the cause of their unease.

In the winter of 2000 a psychic lady spent a night in the Raymond Room. Staff eagerly awaited revelations about their ghostly guests and were disappointed when she left without a word. What transpired that night only the mysterious lady knows but since then none of the ghosts have been seen. Whether they are enjoying one of their restful spells or whether they have departed for good remains to be seen.

When I visited Ockenden Manor in September 2004 I was told that three ghosts had been recorded over the years – the Grey Lady, an old man who shuffled along a corridor, and a young girl. The latter was sometimes seen in the

Elizabeth Room, now a stately bedroom, but at one time part of the attic where the servants slept. There were also reports of cold spots and feelings of a presence.

It has been claimed that one ghost was a servant girl from the 19th century. She used to meet her lover for secret assignations by hurrying along the underground passage from Ockenden House to the King's Head, a busy coaching inn, where he would be waiting. During one of these excursions there was a slight earth tremor and the tunnel collapsed, killing her. There is no longer a King's Head in Cuckfield although the building still stands, occupied today, somewhat prosaically, by a Co-op 'Welcome' store.

EASEBOURNE

Beside the church of St Mary once stood Easebourne Priory, which was founded in the 13th century for ten Augustinian nuns and a prioress. It seems that one prioress (at least) forsook her ideals to live in considerable style at the expense of her sisters. The bishop was not amused and in 1441 ordered her to sell the fur trimmings she so loved to wear and use the money to clear the priory's debts. She was to stop using her sisters as hired labourers and keeping their profit for herself and she was told to make do with just four horses. In 1535 the priory was suppressed. It was rumoured that as the nuns were leaving, the sub-prioress, Alicia Hall, called down a curse of fire and water on the new owners.

Sir William Fitzwilliam took possession of nearby Cowdray Park in around 1535 and received Easebourne Priory in 1536. The following year he was created Earl of Southampton. He died in battle with the Scots and as he was childless his property passed to his half-brother, Sir Anthony Browne, who was granted Battle Abbey in East Sussex in 1538. Another version of the famous 'Cowdray curse' was that it was uttered by one of the monks from Battle Abbey when they too were sent packing.

After a period of some 258 years it seemed that the curse was activated. On 24th September 1793 a fire completely destroyed Cowdray House, the Tudor mansion that had been built by Sir Anthony Browne. The house was in the process of being renovated while the young 8th Viscount Montague, a descendant of Sir Anthony, was abroad and a workshop had been set up in the North Gallery – it was there that the fire started. The alarm was given at around midnight and the villagers of Midhurst rushed to the site, helping to salvage as much as possible. The irony of the situation was that the estate owned its own fire engine, which was stored in a round tower, but in the chaos nobody could find the key to the door. The ruins continued to smoulder for two weeks.

The 8th Viscount, on holiday in Germany, had no idea of the disaster at home when a week later in October he took it into his head to try to shoot the rapids of the Laufenburg Falls on the Rhine. His servant warned him earnestly of the danger but was ignored. The servant even went so far as to lay a restraining hand on Montague's shoulder but the young hothead shook him off so violently that the collar of his coat was torn. The Viscount and a friend set off in their boat, which soon overturned, pitching them into the turbulent water – they both drowned.

Thus 'passes in fire, water and sorrow the glory of Cowdray Castle'. The ruined house was never rebuilt, indeed the family virtually abandoned the site. Some fifty years after the fire a report to *The Antiquary* noted that 'the calamity had palsied the surviving owners'. Not everything had been destroyed and there were still confused stacks of furniture stored in the kitchen, not to mention valuable old documents bundled into the dovecote and left to rot. Nothing was done and ten years on, the situation was just the same. Thomas King from Chichester was so angry at the neglect that he removed some documents for safe keeping while sadly noting that others had been used for kindling. Eventually, some parts of the building had to be demolished as being unsafe. It was left to a family not connected with the ill-fated descendants of Sir Anthony Browne to undertake a certain amount of restoration work.

Meanwhile, one last dreadful event occurred. After the 8th Viscount Montague's death the estate passed to his sister Elizabeth Mary, who married William Stephen Poyntz in 1794. In July 1815 while the family were taking a holiday at Bognor, Mrs Poyntz looked out of her window and watched her husband, two sons and a boatman enjoying a boat trip. Suddenly the boat capsized and the boys, aged ten and fourteen, drowned. Mrs Poyntz died in 1830 and her husband ten years later. Not surprisingly, their three remaining daughters decided to sell the estate.

FULKING

I t is said that parts of the Old Farmhouse date back to the 12th century. The ghost is a devout white-haired lady who was so attached to her Bible that she still carries it about the house with her. Legend has it that she only reveals herself to those she wishes to protect. During the Second World War seventeen Canadian soldiers were billeted at the house. They all saw the ghost and they all survived the war.

GATWICK AIRPORT

Gatwick Airport must be the most restless place in Sussex, with millions of people flying in and out during the course of a year and thousands of members of staff to cope with all the comings and goings.

It is hard to imagine what the site looked like at the beginning of 1930 when it was nothing more than low-lying land regularly swamped by the River Mole. The first airfield licence was granted in August 1930 but it was the third owner, Maurice Jackaman, who really started the place humming. His company drained the land and diverted the river and then they built the circular terminal, which has been popularly called the Beehive ever since. It was fitted with the latest equipment and for the convenience of passengers there was an underground passage linking the airport to the railway station. A grand opening ceremony was held in May 1936 and the crowds were treated to a military display as well as the sight of various aircraft.

Modern technology pushed the Beehive into the background because state-of-the-art equipment was housed in a new building, but it remained in use, albeit for storage and for offices. It was in the Beehive, during the 1980s, that the ghost was seen.

On one occasion a staff member was working late when he began to feel decidedly chilly. This was despite the fact that the heaters were still on. He happened to glance over his shoulder and saw a man in a long, dark coat. Startled, he shouted, 'What are you doing there?' But even as he posed the question he realised he could see straight through the figure to the fire extinguisher beyond. Another time the ghost was spotted at the far end of the hangars. He must have looked real because when he disappeared from view behind some shelving, staff began searching that part of the building. Of course they did not find anybody.

One of the office workers who saw the ghost later identified the figure from photographs of Gatwick in the old days as Sam Gordon, a former airport boss. The feeling was that the old manager was still at his post, patrolling the building to make sure all was well. It was said that he had a fear of fire and went on his rounds to check there was no outbreak. Gordon worked at the Beehive from the opening year of 1936 until his retirement in 1955. He died four years later at the age of 69. When the story appeared in the *Evening Argus* in April 1988, reporters contacted Gordon's son but he could throw no light upon the matter at all. He also stated that to the best of his knowledge his father had no phobia about fire. The few staff members still working at the Beehive in 1988 were reluctant to talk about the ghost and by the end of the year all the first-hand witnesses had left.

Nigel worked at Gatwick Airport in the early 1990s and he had an odd experience concerning a Tri-star plane. It was rumoured that one of the seats at the rear of the aircraft had been recycled from another plane, which had crashed. It seems the seat also brought a ghost along with it. Two or three cleaners reported that when they went aboard to start work they were aware of a shape or presence sitting at the back. But on walking the length of the plane there was nobody there. As supervisor, Nigel had the task of inspecting the plane after the cleaners had finished. One night he went aboard on his own and as he moved down the plane, the lights dimmed one by one, just as if the plane were taking off. The back of the plane was U-shaped and the cleaners had left the five toilet doors wide open for ease of inspection. One by one the doors banged shut by themselves and at the same time Nigel felt a blast of cold air down his back. As he related later with a laugh, he did not hang about.

GORING

On 30th December 1925 George Lewis and his wife had enjoyed a convivial evening at the Downsview Inn in West Worthing and were walking back to their home at 2 Sea Lane when Mrs Lewis saw an apparition. The couple were halfway down Goring Lane and Mrs Lewis was convinced that there was an angel moving ahead of them. She asked her husband if he could see the angel too. He could not and he laughed at his wife's story, blaming her fancy on their night out at the pub. But Mrs Lewis was sure that the angel remained in front of them as they arrived in the village and that it then continued straight on through the lodge gates of Goring Hall and into the avenue of ilex trees. She was so convinced of her sighting that she told her neighbours the Prescotts that same night. The Prescott children were asleep upstairs but woke up on hearing the commotion below, and the accompanying laughter because nobody believed Mrs Lewis's story.

Next day the village was abuzz with the news that Major William Lyon of Goring Hall had died the previous night, just before midnight. He was buried near the south wall of the church tower.

* * *

Some parts of the Bull Inn date back to the 16th century and the original walls are around 3 feet thick. Like other ancient inns, it was sometimes used to store dead bodies before burial because the taproom was held to be the coolest place in the village. The inn was also the venue for inquests. One was held in 1890 and the jury and witnesses were so moved by the plight of the widow that they left their fees for her use. In the summer of 1907 an inquest was held into the

The Bull Inn, Goring.

deaths of two young men, Sidney and Frederick, who had been struck by lightning as they sheltered under a tree. Such was the force of the lightning bolt that their boots were torn to shreds and a penny was fused to a halfpenny and driven 6 inches into the ground.

The Bull Inn has a reputed ghost with precise habits for he is supposed to walk across the floor above the bar at 6.50 pm precisely. However, sceptical Roy Saunders, a previous landlord, favoured a more prosaic explanation – air locks in the hot water pipes. But if that ghost is discounted there is a report of another one, a male figure in shirtsleeves with braces holding up his trousers. Could this be the ghost of a one-time landlord who died after falling downstairs?

HAYWARDS HEATH

Butler's Green House stood on the lane leading to Cuckfield. It is now converted into flats, but, many years ago, a little girl lived with her mother and father in the groom's cottage in the stable yard as her father earned his living as groom to the folks in the big house. Originally, the way to the bedrooms was by means of an external staircase, as was often the case in old cottages. Interestingly, when the quarters were modernised and a new staircase constructed inside the house, the outline of the old staircase could still be detected on the outside wall.

One December night, the little girl heard some ghostly sounds and although her mother reassured her and said she must have been dreaming, this cannot have been the case because she heard the same thing for several Decembers running and once a visiting friend had the same experience. Galloping hooves came gradually nearer and then clattered into the stable yard. There was a pause while the rider dismounted hurriedly and then came the sound of heavy footsteps running up the old steps outside the cottage wall. After an interval the footsteps stumped downstairs, the horse snorted, its hooves struck the cobbles as it was turned around, and finally horse and rider galloped off into the night.

HORSHAM

N o church could have a finer setting than that of St Mary the Virgin set at the end of the Causeway. The spire can be glimpsed in the distance and the visitor is conscious of the many pairs of feet over the centuries that have stepped along this route. Even before the present church was built, people passed this way because of the ford over the river.

A churchyard is rarely the scene of a haunting because people buried in consecrated ground with proper rites are supposed to rest in peace. But there is a portion of St Mary's churchyard that was never consecrated – it was reserved for the unfortunate convicted men and women executed at Horsham.

There have been reports of a spirit here over the years but the best sighting

The Causeway, Horsham, with the spire of
St Mary's in the distance.

would seem to imply there was no connection with dead felons. This encounter occurred in the 1940s and the witness was the vicar. Late one evening he had checked the security of the church and was drawing near to the north porch when he suddenly felt he was not on his own. He glanced around but there was nothing to be seen until suddenly he made out something dark emanating from the crypt. It drifted upwards and materialised into

St Mary's churchyard in Horsham – the entrance to the crypt can be seen just beyond the three tombstones on the left.

the figure of a monk. It moved over the pathway and up the Causeway. But as it reached the vicarage wall, it vanished. Although there was no monastery at Horsham, perhaps the monk was connected with the chantry (now called the St Nicholas Chapel), which is close to the crypt.

HURSTPIERPOINT

The children loved him. It did not matter how often they heard the same tunes grinding out of the barrel organ – they always rushed to see Jacko. The organ grinder was a bent old man whose sole companion was his monkey. He dressed Jacko in a red military-style jacket complete with brass buttons and tiny epaulettes. On Jacko's head perched a jaunty pillbox hat. The clothes were not mere decoration but also served to keep him warm in the winter when they were out in all weathers. Jacko found the cold London fogs particularly depressing; his little face would take on a wizened look while his eyes grew dull. But in the summer he was a different creature, chattering away and taking his hat around the spectators for them to throw in their pennies. When the old man pushed the barrel organ through the streets, Jacko perched on the side with his tail curled like a thin snake around the handle.

When the organ grinder became too old to work, he went to live in his sister's house in Hurstpierpoint, taking Jacko with him. It was one of those solid Victorian edifices and the little monkey's great delight was the bedroom's deep window-sill. It was also something of a suntrap and here Jacko liked to sit, watching what was happening in the street below. He still wore his little red uniform for he was greatly attached to it. He was warm and happy and well fed. Perhaps not surprisingly, when he died, he refused to leave the premises and his ghost continued to perch on his favourite window-sill. People who caught a sight of him thought he was an escaped pet as he was so solid looking. They did not realise it was the organ grinder's monkey, dead these many years.

* * *

Danny, to the south of Hurstpierpoint, is a house steeped in history. The earliest section – the east front – was built in 1582, while the south front dates from 1728. The red bricks used in the construction came from kilns sited by the lake and the façade is ornamented by diapers of blue brick.

George, Lord Goring, was a staunch Royalist and indeed he became a general in the King's army. In 1641 Charles I created him 1st Earl of Norwich. Goring lived comfortably and very happily at Danny, which his grandfather had built. But the Civil War changed everything. Sussex folk mainly supported the Parliamentary cause, with just isolated members of the gentry backing the Royalist side. In 1652 Goring was obliged to sell Danny together with the estate of 420 acres, and the Courthope family purchased it from the Commonwealth.

Henry Campion married the heiress of Peter Courthope of Danny. His grandfather, Sir William Campion, was also a Royalist in the Civil War, although his decision to follow the King's cause had not been easy – indeed he had prayed daily for two or three months for God to direct him on his course of action. His great friend was Colonel Morley of Glynde, who was the Sussex leader of the Parliamentary side. Sir William was killed at the siege of Colchester.

In the 20th century Simon Campion recalled his childhood spent at Danny. He used to enjoy playing in a large room in the north wing and sometimes the children would see a ghost resplendent in full Cavalier costume. Most probably it was Goring, still unable to get over the loss of his beloved Danny.

Danny also has another ghost – this time a pale lady to contrast with the dashing cavalier. She stands at the head of the staircase in an endless wait for a lover who never returned because he had been killed, either in battle or in an accident. People working at the house have reported several sightings in the past.

MIDHURST

The Angel Hotel in North Street is said to have been so named by the Pilgrim Fathers, who were suitably grateful for the inn's hospitality as they made their way to board ships to take them to a new life in America. Apparently, they bestowed the name 'Angel' on every inn prepared to receive them.

But the haunting of the inn is not thought to be anything to do with the Pilgrim Fathers. It is more likely to be connected with the fact that the upstairs drawing room was once used as a courtroom – a practice that lasted until 1848. No doubt the old walls listened to many a tale of woe and although no ghost has been seen, some visitors have complained of an icy coldness in the room coupled with a feeling of unease. Another Sussex inn with a similar history and haunting is the George at Hailsham.

* * *

Many old buildings throughout the country lay claim to a visit from Queen Elizabeth I but the boast of the Spread Eagle Hotel in South Street is genuine

The Spread Eagle, Midhurst, in the 1920s. (Picture courtesy of Robert Jeeves)

for the Queen did indeed spend time here on her visit to Cowdray in 1591, looking out over the market square to enjoy some of the elaborate festivities mounted in her honour.

A Golden Lady is said to haunt one of the oldest rooms in the hotel, which also contains the Queen beam – quite literally the mainstay of the original house. A young woman wearing Tudor costume inhabits the lounge bar, while in the 1980s a maid at work in the bedrooms was startled to see the figure of a coachman suddenly appear and vanish before she had time even to gasp.

PETWORTH

The ghost of a mounted soldier clad in armour used to be seen in the environs of Petworth. He must have been an officer since he rode a fine grey horse, and it was thought that he had been killed during the Civil War. It seems probable that he belonged to the Parliamentary side as the great families at Petworth House and Knepp Castle supported the cause. The soldier was sometimes spotted in Charlton Forest and at other times he was seen riding about the farm at Sokenholes, to the south-west of Petworth, on bright moonlit nights. There was a tradition that anybody sitting up late alone in the farmhouse, might receive a visit from the grey horse – but without the rider. The witching hour was midnight and on one occasion the elderly farmer, a Mr Drew, who had got home late from Petworth Market, actually felt the horse put its nose over his shoulder.

* * *

Hunger's Lane was once popularly known as the Haunted Lane and, in the early 19th century, it was a delightful spot, especially on a hot summer's day when the tall trees growing from the banks on either side formed an arched roof. In the green gloom small shafts of sunlight patterned the path like pieces of broken mirror. In the spring, primroses carpeted the banks and there were also harebells and celandines. The farmhouse of Rotherbridge was at the end of the lane, perched high up on sandstone rocks.

But nobody liked to go down the lane at night and horses picked up on the spooky atmosphere and refused to move. One night the head carter at Sokenholes Farm was travelling back with his young son after delivering a load of corn to Chichester when the horses stood stock still in the Haunted Lane. The animals started to shake while the sweat poured off them like rainwater. The carter lashed them with his whip but they still refused to go forward. He later reported that this had happened to him more than once.

On another occasion a couple had been to spend the afternoon with the wife's father and returned home through the lane late at night. The stable lad who waited up to see to the horse said he could not say who was shaking the most – his master or the horse – and as for the lady she was 'all in a totter'.

Eventually, a man 'skilled in such matters' was summoned to lay the ghosts. It transpired that the unhappy spirits could not rest because their bodies had been placed in a shallow grave in the lane. It is thought that smugglers had murdered them. As soon as the skeletons were discovered, and re-buried in consecrated ground, peace returned to the lane.

PYECOMBE

Pyecombe was once famous for its distinctive shepherd's crooks, and for the lead font in the church. Now it has a rather unenviable reputation as a notorious accident black spot on the A23. There have been many traffic accidents there – a horrifying one occurring in May 2004 when eight people died.

In 1968 Michael Dawes and his wife, from Withdean, were driving home from Crawley with two friends. Michael was driving when he suddenly saw a figure clad in a white trench-coat style of raincoat run across the road to the central reservation. Then she disappeared. He knows he did not imagine the ghost because his wife and one of his friends also saw it. But at the time they thought it might have been a trick of the light and so did not mention the sighting until 1976 when they came forward after reading about another couple's experience.

They were Londoners Patrick Geary and his wife June, travelling from Wimbledon to visit friends in Brighton in early December 1976. Both of them saw a pale figure step into the road and glide across the bonnet of the car before disappearing. It was an alarming experience because if it had been a real person, it would have been impossible to avoid a collision.

Several sightings by unidentified people have recorded that the female ghost has long blonde hair and in one sighting she was said to be limping along the side of the road. Nobody knows the identity of the girl although the general theory is that she was the victim of a traffic accident in the 1960s – some say a motorcycle was involved.

Just to complicate matters further, in January 1977 a Mr and Mrs Wright were driving along the road near Pyecombe when their headlights picked out the figure of a man in shirt-sleeves staggering across the road. He looked dazed and pale and passed so close to the car that they thought they must have hit him. Fearing that the unfortunate man had already been involved in a road accident, Mr Wright reversed his car to look for the stranger but there was no sign of him. They described the experience as eerie. It should be noted that this sighting took place at night whereas sightings of the girl occur at twilight.

In June 2004 it was revealed that famous model Katie Price (Jordan) who lived in a house near Poynings had complained of being followed by the ghost of a young man wearing a tattered shirt. She asked ghost-buster Andrew Green for assistance and he concluded that the haunting was probably linked to a fatal accident on the A23.

RUSPER

In October 1987 it was reported that Mrs Kim Welton, the then landlady of the Star pub, had a theory about the recent sighting of a ghost in the pub. A strange shadow had been observed sitting on a bar stool. On one occasion all the lights suddenly went out with no logical explanation, and there was also some bother with the beer lines. Before she took over as landlady, a plaque had been uncovered on the wall of the main bedroom. It appears to celebrate the birth of eight children to a Mrs Moore – most probably in that very bedroom – between the years 1750 and 1769. Among the children were Mary, William, Elizabeth, Joshua, Joseph, John and James, with sadly, the eighth name being undecipherable. The plaque had been concealed for many years, and it seems often to be the case that when old rooms are altered, fireplaces unblocked or, as in this instance, some hidden artefact uncovered, that some psychic energy is released.

SHOREHAM

In August 1990 Brian and Gillian Eastoe took over the Schooner pub in the High Street and moved in with their children, 12-year-old Christopher and Jennifer aged 8. It is not clear whether or not people had noticed a ghost on the premises before but Gillian saw a female figure in the cellar and her husband could sense the presence strongly. A spiritualist was of the opinion that a spirit was manifesting itself through their daughter.

In fact the atmosphere became so spooky that a month or so after their arrival they sought expert help from some psychic people. One Saturday night they gathered together at the pub to see what could be done to help. It was startling when one of them collapsed on the floor and became to speak in a childish voice. It transpired that there were two spirits – an 8-year-old girl – the same age as

Jennifer, it should be noted – and the girl's nanny aged 26. Apparently, they had both drowned in the cellar when there was a sudden flood. The poor young woman kept on repeating that she wanted to go home. An exorcism was recommended.

High Street Bar, Shoreham, July 2004, formerly the Schooner, now the Ship.

It is not clear whether or not any such ceremony took place but strange occurrences continued. By 1995 there were new managers – Philip Dodd and Shirley Fraser – but they only stayed for eight months. However, during that time, late one night Philip encountered the ghost of a red-haired girl of around 7 or 8 years of age seated on the floor by the front door of the bar. As he watched in astonishment, the girl gradually faded from sight.

There were also reports of a woman in black standing well back from the bar. Philip was told about her and she was also seen by young Jordan, the son of the next managers, Ron and Jenny Hamilton. Jordan developed the curious habit of holding long talks with a girl called Rose. He could not understand why his parents could not see her while he could.

Today if you search for a pub called the Schooner, you will not find it. This is because it was renamed the High Street Bar and is now the Ship. It seems to have distanced itself from its ghostly past.

* * *

The bell from HMS Shoreham inside the Adur Civic Centre.

Nothing could be further away from the popular idea of a haunted building than the modern red brick slab of the Adur Civic Centre. It was built partly on the site of St Aubyn's Street and Albion Cottages, and partly on the site of a theatre. The latter, called the Coliseum, was erected during the First World War to entertain troops undergoing training at Shoreham Camp and was later converted into a cinema.

However, cold spots and doors that swing open on their own have been reported. A green-clad figure has been glimpsed at times and it is suggested that the ghost is a former caretaker of the cinema, wearing his green overalls, who died there in an accident when he was electrocuted. But the most unusual aspect of paranormal activity concerns the ship's bell, from HMS *Shoreham*, that hangs in the reception area around 10 feet above floor level. On occasions it has been heard to ring while there is no sign of movement from clapper or rope. One evening in 1996, during an event at the civic centre, there were loud peals from the bell. People were sitting directly under it and anyone attempting to pull the short length of rope, which is well beyond normal reach, would have been seen. Furthermore, in the autumn of that year Ben Charman, presenter of Coastway Hospital Radio, was alone in the building when he heard a series of muted taps on the bell.

SLINDON

Margaret Aldred saw the ghostly White Horse of Slindon in the 1930s and a lady wishing to remain anonymous and referred to as Mrs Y saw it in around 1936. Mrs Y was walking towards Slindon and was on the verge of entering the wood on her way to Mill Lane, when she turned to look at the view. She was startled to see a white horse galloping up the part of the hill called the Home Gallop towards Bignor. As a horsewoman herself, she took a special interest in the sight and realised that the horse was riderless. She watched it intently as it sped over open country and then it suddenly vanished, with no cover to account for its sudden disappearance. There must have been strange vibrations emanating from the vanishing place on the Home Gallop which other horses could pick up. When she was riding there herself one day, Mrs Y's horse stopped abruptly, refusing to go forward, and she was obliged to make a long detour. On another occasion, her horse bolted at the very same spot for no apparent reason. When Margaret Aldred saw the white horse, it did not have a rider either.

Mrs Y also affirmed that the sounds of galloping hooves were frequently heard in broad daylight without any horses being seen. This would occur quite often in the woods leading to Bay Coombe or in Mill Lane. Once the sound of hoofbeats was so loud and so real that she instinctively moved to one side and actually felt a rush of air as they passed. Corroboration came when Mrs Y and a friend were taking a walk on the Downs. Hearing the sound of hooves behind them, and because the friend was nervous of horses, they withdrew into a nearby field to allow the riders to pass unimpeded. The hoofbeats drew level with them, passed by and the sounds faded into the distance but no horses were seen.

Mrs Y lived in a haunted house in Slindon. Playing the piano one afternoon, she turned to say something to her mother, who was sitting on the sofa, when she saw between them a large and substantial female figure – a homely body, not at all frightening – wearing a long dark dress. It transpired that someone of this description had died in the house, and her ghost had become upset when the cottage was enlarged and renovated and the staircase moved. From then on at any time after 11 pm the sound of footsteps could be heard, shuffling along the passage and going down stairs that were no longer there. The family used to make sure that they were securely inside their bedrooms well in advance each night.

STEYNING

The façade of the Old Priory off Vicarage Lane looks deceptively modern from the road but in fact parts of it date back to the 15th century. It was formerly Steyning Vicarage but today is a private residence, renamed the Old Priory in deference to the monastic foundation that once occupied the site. In the first half of the 20th century the house was known to be haunted and was sold at a reduced price because of it. Fortunately, the mother-in-law of the new owner had spiritualist beliefs and mediumistic friends and together they began to unravel the cause of the haunting.

On their first visit they wandered all over the building and ended up in the

A drawing dated 1844 of Steyning Vicarage, now called the Old Priory.
(Courtesy of Steyning Museum)

cellars discussing the history of the house. Suddenly one of the group felt taken over by a military person and began marching up and down in an agitated state with an overpowering feeling of not being able to escape. It was later discovered that a young soldier had been battered to death down there.

However, the group sensed that there was another unhappy spirit in the house whom they had not yet reached. A week later they returned and held a séance in a first-floor bedroom overlooking the back lawn. The troubled soul was a girl called Lucy who had lived in the house with her parents during the Civil War. She was obsessed with a young man named James, who was fighting in other parts, and she spent all her time looking out of the window for his return. She was in such a sensitive state that even the birds singing in the garden seemed too loud for her. But James did not come back, no letters were sent and in the end she lost the will to live. It might seem odd that all the prayers offered up from the Vicarage over many years could not help Lucy. But as Abdul, the spirit guide, explained, the prayers were too high for her – she was wrapped up in her own misery and needed someone on her wavelength to reach her. Abdul helped to rescue her, praying in an unknown language before encircling her with his arms. The medium saw them moving away surrounded by white-robed figures. Three months later, in August, at a home meeting the spirit of a young girl with curly hair hanging over her shoulders, wearing a poke bonnet and a long gown, came to say thank-you for helping Lucy to link up with her own people. It was Lucy's sister and Lucy was happy at last.

* * *

Peaceful-looking Chantry Green has a rather horrible association because it was here in 1555 that John Launder was burned to death, having been transported from Brighton to suffer as a public example to the people of West Sussex. This occurred during the reign of Catholic Queen Mary, and his 'crime' as a Protestant was listening to the Bible being read in English. Steyning Museum exhibits a copy of an old print showing Launder suspended above the fire with three chains like a roasting chicken rather than tied up to a stake.

Chantry Green House, which was probably built to accommodate the priest who offered Masses at the chantry, has a Tudor core although its façade dates from the 18th century. During the Second World War, it was used as the Company HQ of the local Home Guard and was reputed to be haunted. Peggy Lea lived in a cottage opposite – she had decided to be an unofficial camp follower while her Army husband was stationed in England, having only been married in 1939. Peggy had cause to visit Chantry Green House one day and she took her Scottie dog Donny with her for company. But Donny positively refused to enter one of the rooms and nobody could persuade him otherwise.

UPPER BEEDING

In the year 2000 Ru and Jo were married and went to live in one of Rose Cottages, a group of old houses in the High Street. They had not been there long when one evening in late July/early August Jo smelled something strange. She could not quite put her finger on it but thought it might come from a neighbouring barbecue. A few weeks later Jo had another whiff of the odd aroma but Ru could not smell anything, making her feel rather daft. However, when it happened again – this time much more strongly – Jo made Ru come and stand alongside her because it seemed to be located close by. Thankfully for her peace of mind, this time Ru could smell it too. They pinpointed it as belonging to some type of tobacco smoke. But nobody was smoking in the cottage and the windows were shut. The smell occurred in the same spot and around the same time – 9 pm – and the young couple imagined a previous occupant having a quiet smoke at the close of his working day. They were quite unconcerned and

Rose Cottages, Upper Beeding.

perhaps the ghost felt they were too complacent because he altered his smoking habits – the smell moved to the kitchen and at a different time. Nothing else happened and they laughed off the occasional smell of pipe smoke, sensing that the old bloke was upset because strangers were living in his cottage.

As the place was so small Jo and Ru had bought a sofa-bed to accommodate any visitors, but some friends who came to stay told them that they were woken up during the night by the feeling that someone was sitting at the end of the bed.

By March 2001 Jo was expecting their first baby. The couple were delighted, but it appears that the ghost did not share their joy. One night when Jo needed to go to the bathroom, she found herself rooted to the spot – she just could not get out of bed. Although the bedroom and bathroom were next door to each other, she would have to pass the top of the landing. She had an incredibly strong feeling that there was someone at the foot of the stairs looking up at the bedroom and now that someone was making his way slowly up the stairs. She still could not move and it was not a pleasant experience. After that, the smell of tobacco smoke vanished but Jo remained nervous about getting up in the night. Not long afterwards, the couple moved because with a baby on the way they needed more space.

WORTHING

Everyone has heard of the Jack and Jill windmills at Clayton but there used to be two mills standing just as close together at Worthing. They were situated west of Ham Road (Ham Lane in those days) and about opposite to where the Half Brick pub stands today.

The south windmill was known as Newland's Navarino Mill and, although it was built later than the north one, the term 'Navarino Mills' was applied to both of them. The unusual name comes from the Battle of Navarino, which took place on 20th October 1827. The combined British, French and Russian fleet defeated the Turkish-Egyptian fleet and it was the last fleet action fought wholly under sail. Therefore Navarino is an appropriate name for windmills whose sweeps are often popularly called sails. James Sheppard built the south mill in 1831 and it was the last word in modern expertise. It was five storeys high and worked two stones. The north mill was also interesting because it was an octagonal structure of red brick – quite a rarity in Sussex. It was constructed between 1800 and 1813 for Richard Hide.

The old mill cottages, Ham Road, Worthing.

James Sheppard lived in a cottage close to the mills, and at the time this was quite an isolated spot. The mills continued in use until the last owner, William Barker, died in 1896. They were demolished in around 1909.

However, the cottage remained. Originally, there were two separate dwellings but some time before the 1940s they were converted into a single unit but with two staircases. In the 1990s Lynne, Michael and their children lived in the cottage and they soon became aware of a ghostly presence. It is relevant to describe the layout of the house in order to visualise the ghost's habitual route. The lounge and dining room faced east while the kitchen, which extended to the length of the other two rooms, faced west and occupied the dividing line, as it were, between the two old cottages. There was an interior window between the kitchen and the lounge, and the wall below the window was around 3½ feet in height. The height is important because although the ghost was seen several times it was never viewed as a full-length figure – just the head and shoulders were glimpsed through this window. Lynne had the impression it was a female ghost because it was small-framed and there was a light, grey veil or similar head covering hanging down behind the head. She thought it was probably someone elderly as the figure seemed somewhat stooped. The ghost's route never varied and it always walked from the north side of the cottage to the south at dusk or in the evening.

Sensitive people told Lynne that the atmosphere in the north part of the house was different, not quite right somehow. The ghost was not sinister and there were no sounds but it was still unnerving whenever the uninvited visitor was around. When she saw the ghost, Lynne would feel the hair rise on the back of her neck, goose bumps covered her arms and there was a peculiar tingling sensation behind her ears.

Michael describes himself as a down-to-earth journalist and an unlikely sort of person to see ghosts in the normal course of events. On one occasion he was sitting in the lounge reading when the rest of the family was out and he became aware of a movement past the interior window out of the corner of his eye. Not concentrating properly, he thought it was Lynne; then he remembered he was in the house on his own. All the usual theories of reflected light, sudden draughts and practical jokes to explain his experience have since been considered and discounted.

Lynne and Michael's 13-year-old daughter Maxine was sometimes woken at night when her hair was stroked by an unseen hand. Her parents did not believe her and put it down to an over-active imagination. Some years later they met the former occupants of the cottage by chance and were asked if they had ever noticed that their ornaments had been moved around. They replied to the contrary. Then they were asked if the hair-stroking ghost was still

Maxine photographed at about the time of the ghostly hair stroking.
(Picture courtesy of Michael Sullivan)

active. Lynne and Michael looked at each other in astonishment and when they told their daughter, she was jubilant that she had been right all the time. In fact the hair stroking had gone on for weeks and weeks. Strangely enough, the former occupants' daughter had also been thirteen years of age at the time. She had said to her mother one day, 'That was nice what you did last night, Mum, sitting on my bed and stroking my hair.'

• East Sussex •

ALFRISTON

An elegant-looking house in West Street called Tuckvar, over 200 years old, is home to three ghosts. A contented former resident was a cat that was so attached to a particular spot by a writing desk that he decided not to leave when he died. The animal itself was never seen but sometimes a person sitting down at the desk to write would be conscious of a loud purring.

A grey-haired lady whose dress rustles when she moves has been observed in one of the bedrooms. Perhaps she is a former nanny because she has been known to tuck a sleeping child into bed and bestow a gentle kiss. Not quite such a comfortable presence, perhaps, is the old man wearing a long apron who peers through windows.

BEXHILL

In 1804 Bexhill's population numbered a few hundred people but suddenly, because of the Napoleonic Wars, thousands of soldiers arrived to set up camp. They were not even British but German-speaking Hanoverian troops that became the King's German Legion – George III being also Elector of Hanover. There were four battalions stationed in some 25 acres in the Barrack Road area. The impact must have been considerable and of course at first the newcomers were viewed with suspicion. However, relations soon improved when people realised that the soldiers provided a great deal of employment and the inhabitants also came to relish the music of military bands. Parish records reveal that some local girls married Hanoverian soldiers, while other men brought their families over from Hanover.

When the King's German Legion returned from the ill-fated Walcheren expedition in 1809, the local populace turned out in force to welcome them home to Bexhill. Many of them had perished – not from battle wounds but from the notorious Walcheren fever. The King's German Legion stayed at Bexhill until after the Battle of Waterloo in 1815 when it was re-absorbed into the Hanoverian Army.

Is it one of these soldiers that still haunts the area? People living at

HAUNTED PLACES OF SUSSEX

Chantry Cottage opposite Barrack Hall, which used to be the officers' mess, have seen the tall ghost of an old-time soldier. It is interesting to note that the Hanoverians were at pains to make their soldiers appear as tall as possible by cutting the uniform coat short. Perhaps the cottage was home to one of the officers as it was known to be in existence in those days and was used by the King's German Legion.

* * *

A Bexhill resident, a Miss Luxton, was told by her father about a haunted house in the town but he would never specify exactly where it was, merely stating it was situated in a very long road. The haunting dated back to the time of the First World War when there were several French and Belgian refugees living in Bexhill and the house in question was occupied by a French boys' school. Two of the boys were very homesick and longed to see their parents again. Unfortunately, they decided to swim home across the Channel. Although they were good swimmers they had no idea of the distance or dangers involved. Early one morning before anybody else was stirring, they crept out of the house and hurried down to the sea where they soon plunged in, eager to reach their parents as soon as possible. Their bodies were eventually washed up on the shore.

After the school closed, other people came to live at the house and they complained of strange noises and the sound of footsteps running downstairs. They soon left. The next occupants had a dog that disliked being anywhere close to the staircase – when he did venture near, the hair on his back rose up and he would bark. A possible explanation for the strange, scrambling noises was thought to lie with an infestation of rats or mice. Consequently, a few stairs were taken up for investigation but nothing was found. After that the house became notorious in the neighbourhood as being haunted and as nobody fancied the idea of living there, it stood empty for many years. It was only after the passage of time and fading memories that it was possible to renovate the house and new people moved in. The few people in the know were sworn to secrecy.

* * *

This ghost story is unusual because the details are extraordinarily vivid – so often there is no more than a nebulous shape or the sensation of a presence. Mr M.L. Thorpe, however, saw something much more robust when he was living in a house on Bexhill seafront not far from where the old Pavilion once stood. He was sleeping in a small room on the top floor and one morning in June 1930 he awoke early with the sun streaming through his window and onto his bedclothes. He sat up and saw a figure standing less than two yards away, near the window and at the side of the bed. The figure was of a large and powerfully built man and to all intents and purposes he seemed a living, breathing being, smiling at him and moving his arms. He was dressed in dazzling gold and silver chain-mail from head to foot. His face was visible – except for his eyes, which were shaded by the vizor of his helmet – and he had a long nose, while his smile revealed extremely large, white teeth, especially the two front ones. An enormous chain hung around his neck and it was of an elaborate design. Suspended from the centre was a black cross with an agate in the centre. Mr Thorpe sat and watched the knight for what seemed like several minutes and so minutely did he observe the figure that he gauged the mesh of the chain-mail to be around 1½ inches wide. Then the knight faded away slowly while the chain-mail dispersed in rainbow flashes of light. Mr Thorpe asserted that the ghost was one of the most magnificent sights he had ever seen. His experience was published in an edition of the *Sussex County Magazine* in 1939 and he waited eagerly for somebody to come up with some history or explanation or even corroboration of his story. But there was no response.

So who was this magnificent knight? One thinks instinctively of the Bayeux tapestry, which depicts knights wearing long coats of chain-mail, called hauberks, with a conical helmet to protect their heads. Chain-mail was difficult to manufacture and was usually made of thick iron wire cut into open rings and welded together. A brand new hauberk would probably have glittered like silver. The Bayeux tapestry does show hauberks of two different colours but as both Normans and Saxons wore chain-mail it is impossible to tell which side the Bexhill warrior belonged to. The Normans under William the Conqueror landed at Pevensey Bay in 1066 and travelled eastwards towards Hastings. Possibly they passed through where Bexhill now stands. Alternatively, after the Battle of Hastings the victorious Normans pursued their enemies far and wide and so who knows what desperate fights may have taken place in the vicinity.

BODIAM

Bodiam Castle embodies the popular ideal of what a proper castle ought to look like. Today it is becalmed in its peaceful moat but when it was built its purpose was to guard against possible hostile incursions by the French up the River Rother, which in those days was navigable as far as Bodiam Bridge. Sir Edward Dalyngrydge received permission to build the castle in 1385, only five years after the French had destroyed Winchelsea and eight years after Rye had been laid waste. Sir Edward was familiar with France, having campaigned in Normandy and Brittany.

Bodiam Castle.

In the 1920s Harry Price, the famous psychic investigator, said that sounds of revelry were often heard by people passing the castle at night. The noises included the clinking of drinking vessels interspersed with snatches of songs in a foreign language and the occasional oath. Perhaps Sir Edward had acquired some foreign henchmen on his campaigns. It was also claimed that music could be heard on Easter Sunday. This particular haunting of the castle, however, seems to have faded away completely.

More recently, the sad ghost of a little boy has been reported, seen, for example, by the custodian when he was on his way to lock up the museum one evening in 1994. The youngster's clothes are old fashioned, perhaps dating from the 19th century. It is possible that he fell into the moat and drowned, because he is sometimes seen running along the causeway towards the castle only to vanish halfway across.

BRIGHTON

Arthur Cyril Jefferson Peake was described as a theatrical designer, playwright and former sports promoter. He married an heiress and, although the marriage did not last long, Mrs Peake made her ex-husband an allowance and he opened a flower shop in The Lanes called Fountain Court. Arthur George Noyce was a handsome young man with a mane of blond hair who worked in the shop part-time – he and his mother ran a curio shop in Meeting House Lane. Fountain Court specialised in exotic flowers such as orchids but the prices were far too high and the business soon folded. However, Peake continued to employ young Noyce as a chauffeur/companion.

All went well until Noyce announced his engagement to a pretty local girl. His employer was consumed with jealousy and complained of neglect. On 8th October 1936 the two men dined together in Peake's flat at 33 Brunswick Terrace, Hove. The next morning the maid, Ann Fitzpatrick, carried up their breakfast tray and seeing them both in bed, assumed they were still asleep. Later on she noticed a smell of gas and, on investigation, it was discovered that Noyce was dead with a sash cord around his neck while Peake had made a botched attempt at suicide. At Sussex Assizes Peake was found guilty of murder and on 10th December 1936 he was sentenced to death, the date of execution being set for 11th February 1937. But three days before the sentence was due to be carried out, the Home Secretary issued a reprieve on account of the prisoner's long history of mental instability and he was despatched to Broadmoor instead.

Meeting House Lane, Brighton.

The restless ghost of Arthur Noyce returned to haunt The Lanes. Sometimes he was observed walking towards his mother's curio shop, while at other times he was seen looking through the window of Fountain Court. There was no doubt as to the ghost's identity because all observers described a young man dressed in a sports jacket and sporting a mass of fair hair. The new owner of the curio shop in Meeting House Lane sent the writer Thurston Hopkins a full account of the haunting in the 1950s. One of the ghost's favourite tricks was to hide rare pieces of china, which necessitated hours of fruitless searching. At other times he would sink languidly into the owner's favourite armchair – you could hear the springs creak under his weight – and run his fingers through his hair. The ghost persisted in his old custom of bringing flowers home for his mother. It was never a run-of-the-mill bunch of flowers but rare and fragrant blooms. On occasions the owner could both see and smell the flowers – sometimes the perfume would grow overpowering and somewhat sickly.

One day a very down-to-earth person waited outside the shop for at least 30 minutes because she wanted to discuss private business with the owner but she could plainly see through the window that there was a customer inside – a young man in a sports jacket with fair hair.

It seems that Noyce's ghost disturbed other spirits present in the old building because there were different ghostly manifestations as well – strange lights winking from the devil masks and carved images, bells ringing of their own accord and an elegant white hand pulling back a curtain.

* * *

There have been tales of a monk or a nun haunting The Lanes. One of the best-authenticated accounts was told to L.J. Robinson who used to run a bookshop in Meeting House Lane. His informant was a woman who had been on firewatch duty one night during the Second World War. At that time Brighton and Hove were part of a restricted area, which meant that people were not at liberty to move around freely. The woman firewatcher was therefore surprised to see a hooded figure in Meeting House Lane moving towards the Friends Centre. She called out to the person, who took no notice at all and continued on its way. The woman decided she would have to run after it. But she was astonished when the figure glided through the blocked-up doorway opposite the bookshop.

* * *

Nile Street in The Lanes was named after the celebrated Battle of the Nile, which took place on 1st August 1798. Nelson attacked the French fleet at dusk in Aboukir Bay and destroyed eleven of their thirteen ships. But the history of Nile Street stretches further back in time as the site once formed part of the small ecclesiastical enclave known as the Chantry of St Bartholomew, which came under the jurisdiction of the great Clunaic priory of St Pancras at Lewes. The chantry was established in the 12th century and the Prior's Lodge stood in Nile Street – amazingly it seemed to escape the general destruction when the French razed Brighthelmstone to the ground in June 1514. The chantry was dissolved during the reign of Henry VIII and eventually Brighton Vicarage was built on the site of the Prior's Lodge. Another fascinating detail from the past is that there was once an underground passage connecting the Brewery in Black Lion Street to the corner of Nile Street. Although the north side has been redeveloped in recent times, old houses remain on the south side.

Number 3 is on the south side and is home to a photographic business called First Light, run by Mark and his wife Anna – and by a neat coincidence their surname is Nelson. The décor is light and airy but there have been mysterious happenings such as footsteps heard in empty rooms or on the staircase when nobody is there. Indeed sometimes the atmosphere grows so dark and brooding when Mark is working late that he will say out loud, 'All right, all right, I'm going', and he packs up and goes home. It is as though someone resents an intruder in his house. The television unaccountably switches itself on at times. For instance, one night there was a programme about the supernatural and next morning the television was blaring away although it had quite definitely been switched off the previous evening. Perhaps one of the most bizarre events was the night a whole shelf of books was removed and placed on the floor. The books were not just swept off – and no crash was heard – but there they were on the floor, neatly arranged in the exact sequence they had been placed in on the shelf.

Brighton Town Hall.

* * *

Brighton Town Hall was built in the 1830s close to the historic site once occupied by the Chantry of St Bartholomew. The chapel was situated north of the site and extended into what is now Market Street. All that remains today is the monastery well, with its original stonework covered by a heavy iron grille. It is in the basement

49

of the town hall. The ghost of a monk who died in a fire that destroyed the chantry is said to haunt this area.

The basement is home to the old police cells. There is another ghost there who also has an association with fire. In this case it was a fireplace, which is still in existence. In March 1844 John Lawrence was arrested for stealing a carpet and was questioned by Henry Solomon, the Chief Constable. Lawrence was told to sit by the fireplace while a female witness was fetched. Suddenly, Lawrence got up, grabbed a heavy iron poker from the fireplace and smashed it on Solomon's head with such force that the poker bent. The police chief died the next day, in his fiftieth year. Such was the esteem in which he was held that he was given a public funeral and over £1,000 was collected for the benefit of his widow and nine children. As for Lawrence, he was found guilty of murder and hanged at Lewes. But it seems that Solomon's spirit cannot rest and the ghost of a man wearing a long black coat and top hat has been seen in the basement. There is certainly an eerie atmosphere down there and Fred, the one-time resident cat, always refused to go anyway near.

However, it appears the mysterious atmosphere is not confined to the basement. In July 2004 Pat Dines, the Mayoral Secretary, told me about doors opening by themselves. Her workplace is part of a suite of three inter-connecting offices and several times her door has been opened as if by an unseen hand. A sceptical colleague put it down to a draught until one day when she witnessed it herself – she then changed her mind.

* * *

Parts of the Druid's Head pub in Brighton Place are said to date back to 1510. In later times this venerable building became a coaching inn and was much frequented by London carriers. It takes its name from a circle of stones that once stood in the area, which was popularly associated with Druids in Victorian times. It gained its first licence as a beer house in 1830.

When the writer Thurston

The Druid's Head, Brighton Place.

Hopkins visited the Druid's Head in the 1920s he met a marvellous old character with a red face, elf-like eyes, a beak of a nose and a battered panama hat clamped on his head. It turned out that he was a dowser, or water diviner, who also had the ability to find lost articles. Hopkins stood at the bar groping for his matches – he had fourteen pockets and he could not remember where he had put the box. A low voice told him to try his hip pocket and the dowser also knew the lost article was metal and nickel-plated. After a long conversation the dowser left the pub with a light dancing step and Hopkins felt that there was a strange and indefinable quality about him.

In his book *Sussex Pubs*, written in the 1960s, Rodney Walkerley wrote that at the Druid's Head 'there is a ghost (not, I gather, a very active ghost these days)'. Perhaps the spirits were taking a rest because there have been reports of ghostly happenings since then.

Katie McElroy worked as a barmaid during the 1970s and said a mirror by the staircase used to mist over mysteriously on occasions, as though someone were breathing on it. Then there was the behaviour of the lights after closing time – they would dim right down and then return to full strength. The management, concluding that there was a mundane explanation behind the phenomenon, installed new circuits and had the dimmer switches checked over. But this made no difference.

In the 1970s Mr and Mrs Jim Wood were the landlords at the pub. They were well aware of the ghost and would often see glasses moved from one side of the room to the other. They soon grew used to such occurrences but it sometimes proved too much for more nervous barmaids. In 1978 Lionel Joste took over as the new landlord and, unlike some people, he hoped the ghost would soon put in an appearance. He was used to running a haunted pub as his previous one in the King's Road, London had a resident ghost by the name of Tom Ewell. Lionel had been told that the ghost at the Druid's Head was that of a young man killed in the smuggling tunnel that once ran from the cellar to the seashore. Some writers have thought the stories about smuggling tunnels were pure fiction but it is a fact that there were several in Brighton.

It seems there are other shades haunting the pub too. In August 1994 Cindy Wilkie, the barmaid, was busy in the bar serving a customer behind whom a woman in a red dress waited patiently. Cindy could not understand why the barman who was also on duty stood there twiddling his thumbs when there was a customer to be served – the reason being of course that he could not see her. The lady in red soon faded away.

* * *

In 1885 the landlord of the Marlborough Hotel in Princes Street, Mr Packard, died and the business was taken over by his son Tom, who lived on the premises with his wife Lucy and their three children. Tom and Lucy were both too fond of the drink and in addition Tom had a filthy temper. It cannot have been a happy household as Lucy was not interested in her housewifely duties and Tom was often short-tempered with the children and hit them – he assaulted his wife as a matter of course. Finally, in 1900, he went too far, hitting Lucy over the head with a bottle and killing her. Although he was charged with murder, this was reduced to manslaughter at his trial.

It is Lucy who haunts the pub. In around 1976 Eddie Scannell, the then landlord, was clearing up in the bar late at night after all the staff had left. The atmosphere suddenly turned icy cold and he felt something brush past him. He was so shocked that he decided to leave the rest of the bar work until daylight next morning. In 1998, manager Sue Kerslake encountered a misty figure not once but twice.

The Marlborough Hotel.

In 2000 the United Paranormal Research Society verified the ghost's existence after a site visit. A psychic who accompanied them saw a female figure wearing a black dress and jet beads. Perhaps Lucy was proud of her beads because they came across very clearly. Sue Kerslake suggested that Lucy was probably anti-man after her experiences and was more comfortable with female company. Sue often had the feeling of being watched and once she was astonished to see lampshades twirling rapidly. She said, 'It's not scary because she isn't nasty and she's been here a lot longer than me anyway.' Sometimes Lucy turns off lights or shuts off the gas lines and on one occasion an entire shelf of bottles fell to the ground.

* * *

Today the Stag Inn in Upper Bedford Street appears to be stranded in a timewarp because older buildings in the vicinity have been demolished and its neighbours are high-rise flats. The Stag meanwhile continues much as it always has over the years, having been in existence well before Kemp Town was built. The ghost has been around a long time too as it was haunting the hostelry in 1896. His activities seem to fluctuate and sometimes there is a long period of tranquillity, leading people to think he has left at last. The ghost is nicknamed Albert.

In February 1991 landlord Taff Hill was fed up with Albert's antics. It had got to the point where he found it difficult to sleep at night and was thinking of calling on the assistance of a priest. Albert's catalogue of pranks was impressive – perhaps the most bizarre being the time he placed a case containing 24 bottles of mineral water in the freezer and eventually the lot exploded. On another occasion he threw a barrel of beer down the stairs. Albert also had a lot of fun with a heavy fire door, causing it to open and shut in front of bemused customers. One night the entire contents of a barrel of real ale disappeared into thin air. The staff did not appreciate Albert tapping them on the shoulder either.

Then it seems Albert went though one of his quiet spells, at least until Bob Watkins became landlord in 1998. Perhaps Albert was objecting to a change of management. At any rate ghostly happenings were stepped up within a few months of Bob's arrival, with the beer supply being switched off at the rate of

The Stag Inn, Upper Bedford Street, Brighton.

once a fortnight. Albert apparently objected to the new-fangled pub quiz held on Thursday evenings and once sent a loudspeaker crashing to the floor. Neither was Bob's prized collection of glassware exempt from Albert's attentions. It was displayed on a shelf behind the bar and Albert picked up a glass boot, hurling it for a distance of at least 12 feet where it smashed on the floor.

But who is Albert? A medium was of the view that the busy ghost was a landlord from years gone by, while Danny O'Loughlin, another former landlord, thought it was a chef and moreover reported in June 1984 that a male figure wearing chef's clothing had been seen. The general opinion seems to be that the ghost is that of a man who died in the cellar, most probably in an act of suicide.

* * *

On 13th March 1989 the *Evening Argus* carried a small paragraph stating that the old York Ward at the Royal Sussex County Hospital would shortly be flattened to make room for a car park and that staff hoped the resident ghost would find a new home. But it turned out there had been more than one ghost haunting two-storey York Ward, which had once been used as an isolation ward.

The male ghost was not a frightening spectre and he looked so reassuringly solid that patients did not realise he was not flesh and blood. He never sat on the bed but appeared at the end of it. Moreover he spoke to them, enquiring about how they were feeling and reassuring them that they were getting along fine. He usually arrived at around 11 pm, which was rather late for a social call but perhaps he was waiting until the ward was quiet. At least five or six patients gave independent accounts of having seen him. One unusual aspect about him was the brown trilby hat he wore and he was dressed in a dark, double-breasted suit. He was tall and thin and wore glasses. Nurses became aware of the ghost when patients asked about the identity of their kind visitor and they knew that nobody who matched the description had entered the ward during the night.

The newspaper report stirred up memories for Mrs S.H. Norman who wrote in to tell of her experiences. Mrs Norman was on night duty from January to March 1940 and one night she was in an office on the first floor, looking over the relevant notes for the next morning with a senior nurse. They both heard the heavy outside iron door open with its customary loud noise. Mrs Norman went to the top of the stairs to meet the night nurse, as she assumed the visitor to be, making her usual rounds. The night nurse usually arrived at 11 pm but perhaps she was earlier that night. Mrs Norman heard the sound of the door closing, quick footsteps and the swish of a starched apron – then silence. Mrs Norman returned to the office and explained to the nurse that she was sure somebody had just come in. The nurse was quite matter-of-fact about it. 'That was Sister Geer. She died some years ago and she was the sister on this block for many years.' People who remember Sister Geer say she was a tiny woman with a strong personality.

There was also an older nurse still patrolling York Ward. She was generally known as the Grey Lady because she wore a long grey dress with a white apron – most probably the uniform of long ago. She used to appear and then as rapidly fade away again. Bedside buzzers sometimes went off without being activated and the sound of footsteps in an empty corridor was often heard. But by far the scariest paranormal manifestation was a pair of staring eyes without a face. This was seen by patients and also by a nurse. In fact so many strange events seemed to be happening that eventually a church minister was called in to exorcise the place.

* * *

Housing now occupies a site where the old Bevendean Hospital used to stand in Bevendean Road. It started life in 1881 as a hospital for smallpox patients and they were housed in temporary wooden buildings. By the mid 20th century people thought that smallpox was a scourge of the past but then in 1950 there was an outbreak at Brighton and two patients at Bevendean were confirmed as having the disease on 27th December. Other patients went to Foredown Hospital, Portslade, and to Dartford. At Bevendean a student nurse and a 28-year-old nurse both contracted smallpox and died at Dartford. It was one of these who haunted the hospital. In the 1970s Dr Rose Hunter saw the nurse walking down the corridor and continuing into the kitchen. She must have looked extremely lifelike because Dr Hunter hurried after her, thinking it was a particular nurse she wanted to have a word with concerning a patient. She followed the nurse into the kitchen but there was nobody there. Other staff she questioned knew it was a nurse from the smallpox outbreak because she had been seen before.

By the early 1970s staff nurse Harry Blacklock had worked at Bevendean Hospital for over 30 years. One Sunday morning at midday he and his colleague Sheila James took some specimens to be tested. As they were walking though an alcove they saw a man wearing a blue dressing gown. Harry had just been assigned to Ward Four and he just assumed it was one of the patients. But Sheila knew the patients on the ward and did not recognise him. Harry turned to speak to him and the figure began to fade away 'in a sort of downward spiral'. At the same time Sheila reached out a restraining hand. It seemed as though she caught the man's dressing gown cord, which dropped to the floor. Strangely enough it remained visible on the floor for a second or so after the man had disappeared, then it too faded.

All this was innocuous enough but events took a darker twist in the late 1970s. Staff on duty at night could take an hour's rest break. Quite often nurses and orderlies used the time to have a nap – and where better than on an empty ward bed while remaining fully clothed? One night Harry Blacklock stretched out on a bed at the end of Ward Four at 1 am for his break. It was not long before he was fast asleep. The arrangement was that a colleague would wake him when his time was up. But something got there earlier and he woke up with a fright to feel a weight pressing down on his face – it felt as though somebody was trying to smother him with a pillow. He put up a violent struggle and suddenly he was free. He leapt off the bed, pulled the curtain aside and looked at the ward. There was no sign of his assailant and the patients were peacefully asleep. It could have been a horrible nightmare ... except for the fact that exactly the same thing had happened to his colleague Frank Wilson when he took his break at midnight on the same night and occupying the same bed.

* * *

Judy Cornwell is a well-known actress – one famous television part was as Daisy Onslow, sister of Hyacinth Bucket, in the popular *Keeping Up Appearances*. At the age of twenty she was appearing in J.B. Priestley's *Eden End* at the theatre on the Palace Pier. John Parry, a reporter on the *Evening Argus* went to see the play in order to write a review and that is how they met. They married on 18th December 1960.

Today they live in a house at Brighton dating back to the 1830s. The building is haunted and sometimes John catches a glimpse of two ladies wearing Victorian dress. Judy maintains they are friendly ghosts and occasionally she can hear them talking. But there is one object the ghosts cannot abide and that is a camera. The size or sophistication does not matter to them. When Judy is interviewed, the accompanying photographer is often perplexed at the malfunctioning of his equipment. On one occasion a tripod crashed to the floor, with its legs spread out, in an empty room.

When journalist Angela Wintle interviewed the actress for the *Argus* in 2001, the photographer discovered that 60 of his photographs had just vanished. Judy's comment was, 'Oh dear, they've done it again.'

The ghosts also disapprove of a picture hanging on the wall in the living room. Twice the picture has landed on the floor, splintering the glass. Judy thinks the ladies are unhappy about it because of the artist's racy reputation as well as the naughty inscription on the back of the frame.

But the ghosts are also protective towards the occupants – perhaps they regard them as guests. One evening Judy was sitting up in bed while outside gales lashed the area. All at once her bed shot forward at least four feet. Moments later the wind sent a chimney through the roof to land on the very spot her bed had just vacated.

* * *

Consecrated in 1836, St John the Baptist's church in Bristol Road was the first Roman Catholic church to be built in the area since the Reformation. In the 1930s the parish commissioned the Qualis Photo Company from London to record its interior. The process involved setting up a tripod for the camera and a long exposure was used. When the film was developed, there appeared to be a ghostly female figure wearing a high-waisted dress and a light coloured bonnet encircled with a dark ribbon at the back of the church. The parish priest at the time was so unsettled by the image that he never allowed any of his parishioners to see it.

However, in May 1993 a more broad-minded priest, Father Ian Doyle, decided to allow the picture to be published in the *Argus* as a way of publicising the launch of a £400,000 appeal to pay for repairs to the church. As the ghost was in the vicinity of Mrs Fitzherbert's magnificent memorial, some people like to think it is her ghost. She was buried there in 1837. Sceptics point out that because a long exposure was used, it was possible for a woman to have entered the church and to be caught on film, unbeknown to the photographer. This seems unlikely however as the costume seems to belong to an era long before the 1930s.

St John the Baptist's church, Bristol Road, Brighton. The ghostly figure can be seen at the bottom left-hand corner and above her on the wall is the monument to Maria Fitzherbert. (Picture courtesy of St John the Baptist's church)

Mrs Maria Fitzherbert's liaison with the Prince Regent (later George IV) is widely known but perhaps most people think of her as a flighty damsel. Nothing could be further from the truth – she was a devout Roman Catholic who had been educated in a Paris convent. She married young but was widowed at eighteen when her husband broke his neck by falling off his horse – her second husband died of a chill. So there she was in her twenties, still young and beautiful and twice widowed. The Prince fell violently in love with her but she would never consent to become his mistress and on 15th December 1785 there was a secret marriage. Although circumstances forced them apart, Maria retained a special place in his heart. On his deathbed it was discovered that the King wore a miniature of her and this was buried with him at Windsor. As if to emphasise her virtue, the veiled figure in the church monument displays, for posterity, three wedding rings on her left hand.

BURWASH

The Revd John Coker Egerton (1830–1888) served as curate and later as rector of Burwash for a period of nearly 30 years. He wrote an engaging memoir about Sussex folk, including a couple of ghost stories connected with the parish that had occurred many years previously. His informant was an old lady still alive in 1882 aged 87, who heard the tales from her grandfather (1737–1817) – the hero of the stories.

The scene is set in around 1754 when the lad was some 17 years old. His name was Richard Balcombe and he was a servant at a farmhouse called The Greenwoods on the south-west corner of the parish. One night, quite late, he was obliged to take a message to Burwash, and his route lay over a stile where he was told a ghost was often seen. Accordingly, he armed himself with a stout stave and off he tramped. It was very dark and as he neared the stile sure enough there was the ghost in front of him 'glaring fiercely out of the hedge'. Nothing daunted, he attacked the spectre with his stave. But that was when he experienced a real fright, because as his stave struck home, flames from all sides came flying past his head. He must have been a doughty young man for he stood his ground and discovered he had smashed a rotten old tree stump, which had dried into touchwood, and phosphorous from it glowed in the dark.

On another occasion, Richard was returning home from Burwash one night, carrying a pair of mended boots. Quite probably his previous ghostly encounter was running through his mind when suddenly in the field near the stile he noticed a grey shape that he took to be another spectre. He flung his boots at it. However, the shape was the rump of an old grey horse standing there quite peacefully. But when the boots hit, the horse bolted, taking the footwear with him.

* * *

Rudyard Kipling first set eyes on Bateman's in the summer of 1900 and two years later he purchased it for £9,300 together with 33 acres of land. He claimed that the water-mill was recorded as paying taxes in the Domesday Book and that the new part of the house was built before the *Mayflower* set sail for America. Kipling was delighted with the original beams and panelling of the house, also its staircase of old oak, and was relieved that no Victorian 'improvers' had been at work there. He loved the sense of history, although unfortunately the dampness of the house's situation gave him one cold after another. He liked to spend the mornings in his study and in the afternoons he and his wife, Carrie, went for walks, enjoying the simple events of country life such as watching the progress of ditching and hedging, or listening to nightingales singing from the yew hedges. Yet, as in his poem *If*, he also walked with kings and was a friend of George V. They died in 1936 within two days of each other and it was said the King had died and taken his trumpeter with him.

Today the National Trust owns Bateman's. The most evocative room is the study where everything is just as Kipling left it. There is his old chestnut writing table covered with what he called his working tools – his fountain pens and pen-wiper, his pewter ink-pot and various paperweights – while underneath rests a capacious waste-paper basket. In this room he must have held long conversations with old friends such as Rider Haggard and Thurston Hopkins and here he came to brood when he heard his son was missing at the Battle of Loos in 1915.

It is not difficult to imagine him in this well-loved room but some people have actually seen him still in it, either at his desk, or standing by the window and looking into the garden. The most convincing glimpse of him was in 1975 when John Harvey, a member of the Ghost Club, saw this solid-looking figure in the study. Kipling had such a distinctive appearance that there was no mistaking his identity. Others say that Kipling and Carrie have been seen in the garden where they spent many happy hours designing the layout of beds and hedges, where the pond should go and the places for the lead figures and sun-dial.

It was Kipling who first told Thurston Hopkins about Glydwish Wood nearby, which he felt had a powerful sense of evil. The story behind this haunted place has all the ingredients of high drama. In the year 1828 Benjamin Russell and his wife lived in some disharmony in a cottage and they had taken in a young lodger by the name of David Leany. Times were hard and both men went in for a little poaching. On one of these nocturnal jaunts Russell dropped dead from a heart attack. Leany did the sensible thing and explained to the police how Russell had suddenly died at the edge of Glydwish Wood and how he had concealed the body until it could be moved. But to his horror he found himself under arrest and charged with murder. Gossips had been busy with suggestions that Leany and Mrs Russell were lovers who wanted Benjamin Russell out of the way. To make matters worse, at the trial a doctor testified that Russell had died from arsenical poisoning. Gideon Mantell, a brilliant doctor and geologist of the time, knew something about toxins and suggested to the court that a heart attack was to blame. Unfortunately, Mantell was called away suddenly to attend a patient, and by the time he returned, sentence had already been passed. Leany was hanged, protesting his innocence to the last and threatening to haunt those who had wrongly accused him of the crime. Although it was too late to do anything for poor Leany, Mantell managed to get Mrs Russell's conviction quashed and the doctor to recant his opinion concerning the arsenic.

Thurston Hopkins was convinced that it was the ghost of David Leany whom he and two friends encountered one horrific night in Glydwish. The men had gone to the wood with the object of ghost-hunting but the macabre figure they saw must surely have exceeded their expectations. They heard the noise of something crashing through the woods, accompanied by moans. Then the thing was upon them – a figure with a horribly decomposed face out of which started terrified eyes while its hands clutched at its scraggy neck to try and ease the choking. No wonder the atmosphere in the wood felt evil.

BUXTED

There are only two points of agreement in the stories about Nan Tuck – her name and the fact that she met a violent end. She lived during the 17th century and some say she was a married woman from nearby Rotherfield who poisoned her husband, while others maintain she was an innocent young resident of Buxted who was accused of witchcraft. It was easy enough at the time to label any woman as a witch who happened to be a little bit different from her contemporaries. It only needed one accusing whisper and local gossip would do the rest.

For whatever reason, poor Nan Tuck was terrified as she hurried down the lane that runs between Buxted and Blackboys and bears her name. She ran towards the church of St Margaret, pursued by an angry mob. Perhaps she hoped to find sanctuary inside the church but whether the rabble caught her before she got there, or whether the priest refused to have anything to do with her, the upshot was that she was dragged to the local pond to be subjected to trial by water. The theory being that if she sank, she was innocent and if she floated, she was a witch. Nan survived and fled, drenched and shivering, into the nearby wood. Here again the stories diverge. Some say she was never seen again, others state she hanged herself in despair and her body was discovered the next morning. But there is said to be a record of her burial in 1661 at St Margaret's. If she had committed suicide, her body would not have been buried in consecrated ground and so the grim possibility remains that Nan was lynched. Nan's ghost continues to haunt the lane and her dark shadow can be seen flitting along its edge.

After the Second World War it was decided that the wood should be re-stocked and the planting of saplings was undertaken. But there was one spot where no sapling would flourish, despite repeated attempts. Local people were convinced the spot was associated with Nan.

There was uproar in Hove in the 1990s when pub chain owners Scottish & Newcastle decided to rename the historic Wick Inn on the corner of Western Road and Holland Road. The name chosen was Nan Tuck's Tavern – although this had absolutely nothing to do with the area. Some £350,000 was spent on refurbishment and on providing a Gothic-themed hostelry, with the cocktails named after the Seven Deadly Sins. Nan Tuck's Tavern opened its doors in February 1999. However, the venture turned out to be a dismal failure – perhaps the ghost of Nan Tuck was outraged at the liberty – and only two years later the property was up for sale.

* * *

Craig Davies has his own business working as a pest controller. In an interview published in August 2004 he said he had been to quite a few ghostly places and related the story of how, not so very long ago, he was called to a building in Buxted that had once been the grammar school. He was up in the attic when he noticed his torch kept flickering out for no good reason. At the same time he sensed a cold atmosphere around him. Without warning he suddenly felt a bang on the back of his head as though something really hard had hit him. Not surprisingly, he got out as soon as possible.

CROWBOROUGH

Sir Arthur Conan Doyle and his second wife Jean moved into Windlesham Manor, a large five-gabled house, soon after their wedding in 1907. He was famous as the author who brought Sherlock Holmes and

Dr Watson to life but this was a bitter-sweet triumph because he had invested much more time and energy in his historical novels and was disappointed they were not better received. He had always been interested in spiritualism but his enthusiasm intensified as the result of the First World War because, as he wrote, 'our household suffered terribly in the war'. He lost two brothers-in-law, his brother and two nephews, and his son Kingsley died of influenza in 1918. Jean's friend and bridesmaid, Lily Loder-Symonds, was also an ardent spiritualist and she lost three brothers in the war. In 1914 she stayed at Windlesham. She received many messages from the other side for Jean and Conan Doyle.

With a Miss Besinnet acting as medium, Conan Doyle saw his mother and nephew so clearly that he said later he could have counted the freckles on his nephew's face. His brother General Doyle revealed himself through the same medium. On 7th September 1919 at Portsmouth, Conan Doyle experienced his supreme spiritual moment when, through the mediumship of Welsh spiritualist Evan Powell, Kingsley made contact.

Conan Doyle died in 1930 and was buried in the grounds of Windlesham Manor. If anywhere ought to be haunted, it must be this place and sure enough a ghostly figure has been seen in the vicinity while doors in the house open

Windlesham Manor, Crowborough.

and close of their own volition. Perhaps most interesting of all is the story relating to the period after his death when an important document to do with the estate could not be found and an extensive hunt was under way. All at once Conan Doyle's voice could be clearly heard identifying the place where the missing document was stored.

Perhaps there was a reason for Doyle's restless spirit. In August 2004 it was revealed that the famous author, hitherto regarded as a devoted family man, had in fact been unkind to Mary and Kingsley, the children of his first marriage. Mary ran his psychic bookshop in London but suffered her final humiliation when her father's will was revealed. He left her £2,000 but she was excluded from the royalties that enabled Mrs Doyle and her three children to enjoy a life of considerable comfort.

Today Windlesham Manor is an old people's home and Conan Doyle's body has been removed from the grounds.

DITCHLING

In days gone past, shepherds would have spent many solitary hours tending their flocks of sheep, with a sheepdog as their only companion. Up on the broad sweep of the Downs in the Ditchling area, the only sounds to be heard would have been the tinkling of the sheep-bells as the sheep pulled at the sweet turf, and the song of many birds.

Now and again this idyllic scene would be disturbed and stories about ghostly hounds were told at sheep-shearing time, or in front of a crackling fire in the winter. At twilight, or sometimes later, when the wind was in a certain direction, ghostly packs of witch hounds could be heard running across the skies – with Ditchling Beacon an especially favoured place for these eerie sounds. Nothing was ever seen, but a shepherd with his sharp hearing could make out the noise of the hunt as plain as anything. There was the hunter's horn, the baying of hounds and the thudding of horses' hooves. The cynics said it was a trick of sound (like a mirage when folk claim to see a ship that is actually over the horizon) and that the hunt was really taking place in another fold of the Downs. If a critic piped up that it was an odd time to be out hunting, the cynic had an answer to that too – that soldiers stationed at Brighton were indulging in a little hunting on the side. But to the superstitious, the witch hounds represented nothing less that the hunting of the souls of the damned across the skies.

* * *

Wing's Place, Ditchling, c. 1912. (Picture courtesy of Robert Jeeves)

Wing's Place, an old house situated south of Ditchling church, was sometimes known as Anne of Cleves House. In fact it had nothing to do with that good lady although she did own a manor hereabouts.

Mrs Mary Browne died in 1845 in her 89th year. She was popularly known as Aunt Molly and in her youth ran a small school in the house. The schoolroom was on the first floor and overlooked the road. Whenever there was a wedding or a funeral, Aunt Molly would allow her pupils to gather at the window to watch the comings and goings at the church.

It is amusing to note that when the ancient house was put up for sale in 1894 the advertisement stated that King Alfred the Great built the house and that it was described in the Domesday Book. But they added the caveat 'the vendors do not guarantee the accuracy of these statements'.

After the sale the house was let as tenements and it remained divided up for many years. The haunted part involves a staircase leading to a tiny attic bedroom. Two old ladies were once being shown over the house but they felt that their way up the stairs was physically barred. Other people have heard footsteps, or, more romantically, the rustling of a long, full skirt.

* * *

Mulberry Cottage is in East End Lane and in the 1940s the Lawrences lived there with their housekeeper, a long-standing member of their family circle. Geoffrey Lawrence was an eminent member of the legal profession, becoming a KC in 1950. He was knighted in 1963.

During the war years Mulberry Cottage served both as a home and as a country retreat. Mrs Lawrence supervised the farming activities while her husband was busy in the City.

The cottage had an old-style front door like a stable door and the top half was often left open. The two women used to sit in an adjacent room to await Mr Lawrence's return from London. The first thing they would hear was the click of the half-door being opened, followed by the sound of his footsteps walking across the quarry-tiled floor. It was the signal to start doing something about the evening meal. However, on at least two occasions when the footsteps were heard quite distinctly, the women went into the hall but there was no sign of anybody. The footsteps could not have been imagined because they both heard them at the same time and, besides, the sound of someone walking over quarry tiles is quite distinct from anything else.

Some years later, after they had moved from the Mulberry Cottage, Lady Lawrence heard about a possible explanation for those ghostly footsteps. The cottage possessed a large attic and it was rumoured that a former occupant had hanged himself from the rafters.

EASTBOURNE

The elegant Devonshire Park Theatre was opened in 1884 and possessed two Italianate towers and a stuccoed frontage. The ghost, however, is not of that vintage and moreover he is a musician. He wears the traditional uniform – white shirt, bow tie and tails, and in case there should be any doubt as to his calling, he usually carries his bow and violin. It might seem odd that a musician should be so attached to a theatre but a live orchestra always accompanied the Christmas pantomime. Perhaps he had warm recollections of the place, and there is certainly nothing like an audience of excited young children for creating a happy atmosphere.

In 1968 Geoff Standfield, the theatre electrician, was working alone in the theatre one Sunday morning, checking the spotlights mounted on the balcony. He happened to glance down into the orchestra pit and there in full view was the violinist. But the figure soon disappeared.

In 1987 Steve Gausden, the doorman, was busy locking up after the last performance. The theatre was supposed to be empty when suddenly he

Devonshire Park Theatre, Eastbourne.

noticed a dark figure moving along the front of the stalls and as it passed the brass rail of the orchestra pit, it blocked out the reflected light. Then it vanished. But the exit door was locked. At that time Gausden had never heard about the ghostly musician.

* * *

The famous chalk cliff of Beachy Head rises a dramatic 535 feet above sea level. Although not mentioned by name it seems certain that it featured in an account of St Wilfrid's visit to Sussex in the 7th century when he arrived to convert the people to Christianity – Sussex was the last county of England to become Christian after the Dark Ages. St Wilfrid found the people in the grip of a terrible famine. Life was so hard that older people took to jumping off cliffs so that there would be more food left for the children. St Wilfrid taught them how to fish to avoid such a calamity happening again.

There has been a long history of people falling off Beachy Head and they were not all suicides. Some fell accidentally, others were deliberately pushed. The Revd Henry James, once curate of Ditchling, became vicar of Willingdon in 1843. Seven years later he was taking a walk on the cliffs near Beachy Head with his little daughter and a friend when he ventured too close to the edge; the

Beachy Head.

ground gave way and he fell to his death.

It is said that in 1538 a priest was hiding in a manor house at Birling Gap – this was at the time when people were forbidden to practise Roman Catholicism. But the priest's presence was betrayed to the authorities. He met his death when soldiers flung him over Beachy Head. Some people have reported a priest running along the edge of the cliff, crying for mercy. In the 1940s an exorcism ceremony was conducted at Beachy Head in front of a small group of people. It appeared that the ghost had just been contacted when suddenly the medium started to run towards the cliff edge – he was pulled back just in time. There have also been tales of a black monk beckoning people to their deaths.

Another gruesome story dates back to ruthless smuggling days. In 1750 Thomas Fletcher, an exciseman, was patrolling his beat at night along the cliff, his path being marked by lumps of white chalk to prevent him from going too near the edge. Nearby, smugglers lay hidden in the furze, waiting for a signal from an approaching boat. Perhaps the smugglers moved the pieces of white chalk – at any rate Fletcher missed his footing and went over the edge. But he managed to hang on by his fingertips. When the smugglers discovered this, they stamped on his hands until he let go. He was found the next day, dead on the beach, his fingers broken. He was buried in the churchyard at Friston.

It would be surprising if this spot were not a haunted place, given the number of suicides that continue to happen. A modern alternative to plain jumping is to go over with the car. During the 19th century there were around two deaths a year but the place was only known to Sussex folk. The danger today is that the whole world knows about Beachy Head. The death statistics hover at around 20 a year.

A young woman who committed suicide in the 1850s is also said to haunt the area. The ghost is wearing a long grey dress and she has been seen walking along the edge of the cliff and near the site of an old farm building. Towards the close of 1978 three walkers out for a stroll one evening spotted her and there have been other sightings too.

In June 2004 a very down-to-earth young man was driving with a friend along the A259 out of Eastbourne towards Brighton. They had been working late and it was well after midnight when the driver suddenly spotted a grey hooded shape moving along the grass just near where the road turns off towards Beachy Head. The figure crossed the road in front of him. To say he was astonished would be an understatement because he did not believe in ghosts and neither had he heard that Beachy Head was haunted. It was only after the sighting that he began to make enquiries to see if anybody else had had a similar experience. His friend saw nothing at all.

HAILSHAM

During the 19th century Hailsham Petty Sessions were held fortnightly on market days in two upstairs rooms at the George Hotel – a sitting room and a bedroom; usually there were two magistrates. Offences ranged from highway robbery to poaching and brawls. In 1982 a former manageress at the George reported that one night she had woken up suddenly feeling terribly cold. She glanced at the foot of the bed and was horrified to see the ghost of a gaunt man with strange, piercing eyes staring at her. It was most definitely not a dream because her husband, 'a most sensible person', saw it too. The Angel in Midhurst, West Sussex, with its reports of a lingering 'icy coldness' in an upstairs room, had a similar law-enforcement role in days gone by.

HASTINGS

Mrs Mo Salmon lived at 11 All Saints Street for six years until 1984. It was an old house of the hall variety, subsequently divided into two dwellings. Although Mo never saw the ghost she was made aware of her presence by the lovely perfume she emitted. Mo tried to identify this by sniffing vigorously at all sorts of different potpourris but she was unable to decide on the exact scent. Sometimes she noticed a strong whiff of perfume as she was settling into her bed but it never upset her – she would just wish the ghost 'Good night'.

The first member of the family to be aware of a ghostly presence was the dog – a Great Dane. In the early days, he was frightened and once shot upstairs to hide between the twin beds in a quivering heap. As he refused to leave his hiding place, they covered him with a quilt and left him to recover in his own time. However, this ghost did not confine herself to one room.

All Saints Street, Hastings, with the tower of All Saints' church in the background.

On one occasion the family were quietly sitting in the living room when the latch of the door leading to the kitchen lifted and the door swung open. This could not happen of its own accord or because of a draught, as an extension had been built onto the kitchen.

Mo said the ghost used to let her know she was still around by moving small objects. For instance, she would leave her book on the table before going to bed and next morning she would find it placed on the sideboard. In the early days of living in the house she decided the right way to treat the presence was just to accept it. She said out loud, 'Look, I don't own the house, I'm only here as a temporary custodian.' She even grew quite fond of the ghost.

Some of Mo's friends were not quite so taken with her ethereal visitor. A woman friend came to stay unexpectedly and sat downstairs while a bedroom was prepared at the top of the house. When Mo came down, her guest looked at her ashen-faced, 'Oh, you never told me there was a ghost in the house.' She had actually seen the ghost, which was more than Mo ever had. She described it as a shimmering female form, fading away towards the edges.

* * *

Hastings' White Rock Theatre opened in 1927 and could be considered something of a newcomer when compared with more ancient theatrical structures. However, there used to be a hospital on the site and this may account for the ghostly encounters. In 1972 Barry Hopkins was at the theatre in a professional capacity – he was taking part in a variety show. One afternoon the weather did not look very promising and he thought it would be a good idea to sort out his dressing room. He went through the manager's office and came out at the back of the stalls. The place was in total darkness. All at

White Rock Theatre, Hastings.

once the atmosphere turned chilly and the hairs on the back of his neck stood up. He just knew there was something standing right next to him. He felt he must get away and, running and stumbling, he rushed backstage and was greatly relieved when he came across a fellow performer.

David and Marion Hartley worked at the White Rock in the 1980s; David was theatre manager and Marion ran the bars. It could be that a major refurbishment had somehow disturbed the spirits, but it was some months later that Marion encountered the ghost. One morning she arrived before 8 am to clean the bar pumps. She unlocked the lounge doors and at once saw that the chair in the far corner was occupied by a tall, elderly man wearing a raincoat that had seen better days. At first she did not take too much notice, assuming he was one of the cleaners – then she realised she was the only person with the keys and turned to ask how on earth he had managed to get in without setting off the alarms. But there was nobody there.

* * *

It requires an effort of the imagination to conjure up a picture of Hastings Castle as it was in its heyday rather than the somewhat forlorn ruins that we see today. In its prime Hastings Castle was an impressive spectacle, set in area of some 11 acres and perched on its cliff top above the sea – since those times the sea has receded and part of the cliff has been deliberately demolished to allow

for the expansion of the town below. It is said that *Hastings Castle.*
sometimes a vision of the whole castle can be seen
over the sea with pennants flying from the battlements and the sound of
chanting monks from the collegiate church of St Mary, which was established
within the castle precincts. The chancel arch still stands and often serves as a
focal point in photographs of the ruins. Thomas à Becket, who was murdered
on 29th December 1170, was once Dean of this church and it is thought to be
his ghost that has been observed on occasions in the winter.

However, recent sightings of a ghost have been of a female apparition
cradling a baby in her arms near the cliff edge. Nobody knows her identity but
it seems likely that she committed suicide there.

* * *

The Wishing Tree pub in Hollington started out as a private house and during
the Second World War troops were billeted there. In 1968 John Northwood
took over as landlord and soon he and his wife Ursula noticed there was
something strange about the pub. John was convinced that the place was
haunted by one of the two old ladies who used to own the premises. His
brother from London came to stay and picked up that there was 'something
funny' on his first night – before anybody had mentioned a ghost. The family's
dog howled for no reason that anyone could see and then there was their little
boy Mike, aged two, who stopped sleeping through the night as he used to do.

Instead he was waking up at all hours, laughing out loud. He was too young to be able to explain what was amusing him but he did say there was a funny face, and he tried to copy it. One day a young woman walked into the pub and asked John how they were getting on with the ghost. It turned out that her father, Major Lewis, had been a previous landlord. To the Northwoods' astonishment she related how her young brother also used to wake up and laugh in the very same bedroom.

HERSTMONCEUX

In the 1940s G.H. Brierley was a contributor to the *Sussex County* Magazine. He recounted the story of a Londoner who stayed with friends in Herstmonceux. They lived in a delightful old house with a large garden full of mature trees and the visitor enjoyed taking a stroll outside before turning in. One evening a wind howled outside and the hostess remarked to her husband, 'Listen to that wind – a good night for Old Copping.' When the visitor stepped out for his customary walk he found that the wind had increased and he watched the branches of a large elm being tossed against a background of scudding clouds. As he turned a corner of the path towards the tree, he felt a restraining hand on his shoulder, preventing him from going forward. There was nobody behind him but he felt uneasy and began to retreat. Then he had second thoughts and decided to finish his stroll after all. But at the same place he felt the hand once more. He grabbed at his shoulder and whipped around but again there was nobody in sight. Thoroughly unnerved, he dashed back to the welcome brightness of the house and as he did so a great branch crashed down on the exact spot where he would have been had he not turned back. He was told that 'Old Copping' had saved his life and that many years ago a gentleman named Copping had been the house owner and had been killed by a falling branch in the garden.

HOVE

In 1949 the writer Gilbert Frankau came to live at Hove, occupying a flat on the first floor of 4 King's Gardens. He was the author of several best-sellers (now largely forgotten) but one of his most popular books was called *Peter Jackson, Cigar Merchant*. It was set locally and included descriptions of places such as the Metropole Hotel. He was working on a book at his flat when he died on 4th November 1952. It might be assumed that a writer with a half-

King's Gardens, Hove.

completed book would be a suitable candidate for a haunting. However, it was not Gilbert Frankau who haunted the flat but his wife, who survived him for many years and died in 1985. A lady living in the house had a clear view of Mrs Frankau's ghost on 11th October 1985. She was going downstairs and happened to look over the banisters and there was Mrs Frankau standing outside her front door, as plain and definite as she remembered her. Her figure was stooped with age and she was wearing a grey winter coat that was almost the last new garment she bought. Mrs Frankau had become very frail in her later years and she hardly ventured outside at all – a hairdresser called to do her hair and if she needed to go out, a taxi was summoned.

This is not the only story concerning 4 King's Gardens. In 1982 a couple moved into a flat on the second floor. Instinctively, the woman felt misgivings, picking up an unhappy atmosphere. But her husband thought such feelings were ridiculous and anyway it was only a temporary move. A second couple moved into an adjacent flat on the second floor in 1983. Here again, the woman felt uneasy but she never realised quite how oppressive the atmosphere had been until they moved out and she felt as though a weight had been lifted from her. Once she tried to sell a pair of large and expensive curtains. A woman who came to see them turned out to be a medium and she told her to move out as soon as possible because some very unhappy experiences must have occurred in the house.

* * *

The Old Market in Hove was once a covered market designed for the inhabitants of the Brunswick area. But it was not a success and it was converted into a riding school known as Dupont's Riding Academy. Then, in the 1980s the building was restored and is now an arts centre. In the early part of the decade Mr G. Denney, the director, was in the control box of the small theatre when he was tapped on the shoulder by an invisible hand.

In 1984 Mrs Hilary Wishart glimpsed for a few seconds a soldier's face looking at her through the glass of the office door. But she became rather irritated when he continued to visit because, as she explained. it makes you feel uncomfortable when someone is watching you. On his last visit she marched outside her office and demanded the ghost identify himself. Oddly enough, this seemed to do the trick and she was never bothered again. It may be relevant to this story that when an old counter from Victoria Station, which had been installed in the bar of the old market building during the 1980s, was being dismantled in 1989, an old cap badge belonging to the West Yorkshire Regiment, fell out.

The Old Market, Hove.

There have been reports of footsteps and a strange glow while an unseen presence is apt to jostle people on the stairs. There is also said to be a cold spot by the place where the winding mechanism for hauling heavy items to the different floors operated. The large wheel – some 10 feet across – is still in place and could lift carriages as well as more mundane articles such as coal and fodder for the horses. There are two versions as to why this spot should be afflicted. One story states that a woman unlucky in love hanged herself there while another tale maintains it was a man who accidentally became entangled in the lifting chain and was killed.

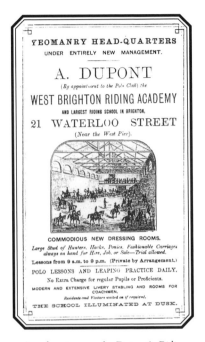

Perhaps the most intriguing haunting belongs to the horses. On three separate occasions in 1996 Stephen Neiman, chief executive of the Old Market Trust, heard the sound of horses. As a boy he used to muck-out horses so he was quite familiar with the sounds associated with them, including the thump of a horse against a stable door. In 1996 Martyn Barrett, the building manager, also noticed the sound of horses on six separate occasions. In June 1999 it was reported that Mr Barrett had been working in the basement when he distinctly heard the noise of hooves being stamped and the neighing of a horse. In June 2004 Stephen Neiman told me that the horses were still active and had been heard as recently as the previous February.

* * *

An advertisement for Dupont's Riding Academy in the former Old Market building. (Picture courtesy of Hove Reference Library)

In 1926 Hove Museum opened in a mansion formerly called Brooker Hall owned by the Vallance family. The museum received many gifts from Hove residents and in 1949 an unusual one arrived in the shape of a large embroidery of an ecclesiastical nature dating from around 1550. It is a composite work with separate panels and strips, and the materials used were coloured silks and metal threads on linen, mounted on velvet. When the embroidery was on display, two girls who had been looking at it left abruptly, saying there were strange vibrations. By the 1980s the embroidery in its massive frame hung away from public view on the wall of the curator's room.

On 4th January 1985 a few people, including the author, visited the museum to see whether it was possible to record the ghostly footsteps that are sometimes heard. As is usual in such circumstances, the ghost decided to have a quiet night. However, the equipment did make a most interesting discovery about the embroidery. As soon as the ozone-sniffer was put in the vicinity of the cross, it began to bleep; sweeps were taken from all four directions and the

Hove Museum.

Detail of the ecclesiastical embroidery, Hove Museum.

reaction was always the same. There was no reaction to the other figures. Then there was the curious fact that the area next to the embroidery registered two degrees warmer than the rest of the room. Possible sources of heat were checked inside the room and on the outside wall too, but there was nothing to explain it, although the type of material used in the depiction of Christ's body may be relevant. This story was mentioned in my previous book, *Ghosts of Sussex*, and not long afterwards the curator removed the embroidery from its frame and put it into storage.

ICKLESHAM

The Queen's Head started life as a farm-house and one can imagine the farmer warming himself on a winter's night beside the huge fireside. In the 1960s the landlord here, Charles Anthony Crundwell, possessed the unusual ability of seeing spirits – having glimpsed his first one at the age of nineteen. Interestingly enough, he said spirits do not look like the traditional idea of a ghost – that is pale and transparent. The spirits he saw looked like ordinary mortals, although they appeared to have stepped out of old sepia-coloured photographs and were surrounded by a golden brown aura.

When a ghost turned up at the Queen's Head to claim his favourite place by the fire, the landlord was able to give a clear description. He saw the figure of an old man sporting sideburns and dressed in rough tweeds with a heavy gold chain looped across his waistcoat. Nobody knew the ghost's identity and so they nicknamed him George. Crundwell thought George might have been a character who died in around 1890 and by all accounts enjoyed a novel send-off. Apparently his coffin was heaved up on the counter while the locals drank to his memory.

Crundwell said he used to experiment with ouija boards in a bid to develop his psychic powers but he would not touch them any more. He told the tale of a lad he knew who lived with two maiden aunts during the Second World War. Sometime after they both died, the nephew's name was spelled on an ouija board, to be followed by the chilling message: 'We have news for you. You will be with us soon.' A few days later the young man fell off a ladder at work.

LEWES

The present Malling House, which today serves as the HQ of Sussex Police, was built in 1710 of grey brick with red brick dressings. It is a handsome two-storey building and inside there is an elegant staircase. The site on which it stands is ancient as there was once an ecclesiastical building hereabouts, which was demolished in the 16th century, at the time of the Dissolution of the Monasteries. In 1947 East Sussex County Council purchased Malling House together with thirteen acres of land surrounding it.

The house is said to be particularly spooky on windy nights when there is creaking and rustling to be heard. A cleaner found one particular cupboard unnerving because the door had slammed shut on her several times and once she had been obliged to call for help. In the end she refused to go anywhere near it.

A secretary saw a woman wearing a frilly cap and a pale dress and strangely enough it did not disturb her as the woman seemed real enough. But just before the sighting the room had grown strangely cold. The ghost is supposed to be Annie, who once worked in the house as a maid. Perhaps she was a pretty girl – at any rate the story goes that she caught the eye of her employer's son and he soon made her pregnant. Unhappily, she was killed in a fall down the stairs and never gave birth to her baby. The fact that Annie haunts the house suggests that the tragedy was not an accident. Annie is also known as the Lady of the Rose Garden, as she used to enjoy tending the flowers.

In 1981, when part of the house served as a communications HQ, PC Paddy Rea was on duty taking night calls. Both he and his colleague felt a ghostly presence and looked up at the same time. Later that night he and another colleague saw a figure glide past the door to the corridor. They went to investigate but there was nobody about.

* * *

Brooman's Lane is one of those delightful, crooked, flint-walled twittens that run from the High Street. In 1992 I received a letter from a man living in Brooman's Lane who had read my *Ghosts of Sussex* and wondered if I knew anybody who could help him. The problem was some frightening experiences in the night, together with scrabbling sounds on the wall. Indeed things had

Brooman's Lane, Lewes.

grown so bad that he could no longer contemplate sleeping in the bedroom and instead paced the streets of Lewes until daylight returned. A neighbour told him that two years previously a lady had died in a fire there.

I replied to his letter but meanwhile he had found someone locally to help him. The medium arrived at the flat and went alone into the bedroom at 1 am with his equipment and lit candles. Half an hour later he emerged with tears streaming down his face. He explained that he had contacted the lady and discovered she had been terrified when she awoke to find the room thick with smoke. When she died, her spirit did not know how to leave. She saw a light but was too frightened to go towards it because in her confused state she equated it with the fire that killed her. The medium was able to help her go forward to the other side and he said it was so beautiful when she found people she knew waiting for her.

The feeling of dread lifted from the flat and although there were sometimes odd noises, it was no longer frightening. On one occasion when the occupant was making a phone call, the whole room became filled with the scent of candles and there was a peaceful atmosphere.

PORTSLADE

Sellaby House, Portslade.

Alice King occupied Sellaby House from the 1870s, along with her brother. She was enabled to live there through the generosity of her late employer Hannah Brackenbury. Alice had worked her way up from housekeeper to devoted companion. When Alice died in the house on 5th February 1901, her executors sold the property to Booth Hay Metcalfe, a retired lieutenant colonel, who in 1913 sold the property for £1,200 to East Sussex County Council. The present owners are Brighton and Hove City Council. The house has fulfilled a variety of functions – health centre, clinic, adult education centre, and a venue for children with special needs.

Joyce Ball worked at Sellaby House for some seventeen years as a receptionist and she experienced the ghost on several occasions. She never saw a figure in the house but often became aware of an uncomfortable presence following her around. It was not exactly threatening but it radiated disapproval – as though she had no right to be there. One weekend she was sitting on her own in the office typing out lists when she became conscious of it right in front of her. She moved to another room – it followed her – she went back to her desk – it was there. At last in exasperation she went to the canteen to get a drink, being followed as usual. She opened the door, banged it shut and locked it and all at once the atmosphere cleared and she was left alone.

The most haunted part was the basement. The room to the right of the staircase was supposed to be the seat of ghostly activity. When this room was converted into a pottery centre it was part of Joyce's duties to set the kilns so they would be ready for classes later in the day, and she was often acutely aware of something evil there. But the only ghost Joyce ever saw was a female figure in the garden early one evening. There were always so many people coming and going that she did not take much notice of this person. But not wishing to appear rude she said 'Good evening'. There was no response and when Joyce turned to see where the woman had gone, there was nobody in sight. The caretaker's wife Dorothy also saw this ghost.

The upper part of the house is used as a caretaker's flat and Vic and Dorothy Hart lived there from 1962 for many years. They had a dog, a whippet-cross, who absolutely refused to go into the basement. He would stand at the top of the stairs with his hackles raised. There were disturbances in the flat too. A large painting of a sunset was removed from its hook and placed at the back of the mantelpiece, although the Wedgwood ornaments in front were not disturbed. Another large picture in the hall was not so fortunate – it was thrown to the ground and the glass smashed. There were other happenings such as the overturning of a heavy table lamp. In the evenings when the couple watched television, the floor would creak and the sofa vibrated gently as though someone were walking around it. Dorothy also felt her head being lightly patted while Vic sat opposite her.

A sound that occurred regularly at 7 pm, 9 pm and 11 pm was the loud slam of the front door, which was adorned with a heavy cast-iron knocker. One evening they decided to keep watch by the stairs as 7 pm approached – dead silence – but as soon as they went back upstairs and sat down, there was the usual bang. At times the bedroom door swung open of its own accord and once the loft door opened on its own – a seemingly impossible feat because it was recessed and heavy. Dorothy only realised it was open because she could hear the sound of rain drumming on the roof. A rather unpleasant manifestation was the foul stench sometimes encountered on the elegant staircase, although this was never noticed beyond the door of their flat.

Eventually, the Harts became fed up with the haunting and sought the help of the minister at Southwick Methodist church. In 1987, after long and careful questioning, he agreed to help. He said special prayers in Sellaby House and it has been peaceful ever since although the odour still recurs at times on the stairs.

* * *

The Stonery was a large farmhouse in north-east Portslade once occupied by the Godsmark family. Samuel Godsmark was a market gardener and he died in

The Stonery, Portslade, in the 1920s. (Picture courtesy of Hove Reference Library)

1829. He was buried in St Nicolas's churchyard, where his gravestone is still to be seen. He and his wife Judith had four sons – William, Henry, James and Owen.

John Broomfield, who was born in 1925, lived in the Stonery for many years as a boy and young man and said the house was haunted without a shadow of a doubt. The family always called the ghost 'Old Mother Godsmark' and thought she may have been the Judith just mentioned. The Broomfields became very used to her appearances and she was never perceived as threatening. However, the family pets reacted differently and nothing would induce the dogs to venture beyond the second flight of stairs. This was especially noteworthy because the dogs were accustomed to follow John Broomfield wherever he went in the house or farm.

The ghost appeared at least once a year during the winter and occasionally three or four times. The Broomfields began to make a note of her appearances to see if they could work out a pattern, but sadly that diary has been lost. Old Mother Godsmark appeared as an old lady in a long gown with loose white hair – in fact she gave the impression of being ready for bed. She also liked to make her presence known by opening doors frequently. These were of the old-fashioned latched variety and there would be a click before the door swung open. More eerie was the sound of a trunk being dragged along the landing when there was nobody up there.

An independent confirmation of the house's haunted status came from the Revd Charles McDonald Hobley (father of the television personality McDonald Hobley), vicar of St Andrew's Old Church, Hove from 1941 to 1951. On one occasion the vicar wanted to see his son on television but there were not many TV sets around in those days. So he phoned Albert Broomfield, John's father, and asked if he could come and watch their set. As soon as the vicar walked in, he went straight past Mrs Broomfield, who being only 4 feet 11 inches in height was used to being overlooked, and strode into the pantry area saying, 'Now this is most interesting.' He had picked up on the atmosphere right away. But Mrs Broomfield refused to let him make any investigations because 'the ghost has never done us any harm and we don't intend to disturb her.'

The Stonery was demolished in the 1950s and it is possible the ghost may have moved house. At any rate, there came a report that a bungalow in North Lane, built on Stonery land, was the scene of strange happenings. David Meaden moved into his bungalow in 1956. He often heard unexplained noises in the loft, the back gate kept opening and closing of its own accord, and there was a smell of wood smoke in the living room. In 1985, he was alone at home watching the television when he sensed that somebody was sitting beside him. He turned and saw an elderly lady facing the other way and wearing what he described as Elizabethan clothes. She remained there for a full five minutes before suddenly vanishing. It was the only time he ever saw her. By 1988, the haunting had dwindled to the occasional smell of wood burning in the living room.

ROTTINGDEAN

In December 1988 the *Leader* reported that the ghost of film star Cary Grant was haunting exclusive Rottingdean Club in the High Street. The story caused great excitement and went around the world. The manager received calls from Australia and from all over the USA; spiritualist groups wanted to hold séances in the cellar, and Cary Grant's niece turned up in person hoping to make contact with her uncle. Apparently, Cary Grant had once attempted to purchase the club and while negotiations were under way he stayed in room nine.

The *Leader* article also

The Rottingdean Club.

described another ghost which was said to be on the premises. The barmaid was in the cellar when she noticed a man in a white coat sorting out bottles. She thought nothing of it, assuming the figure was the manager, and so she just collected what she needed and headed back upstairs. When she reached the bar, she discovered that the manager had been upstairs all the time.

RYE

The Mermaid Inn boasts that it was rebuilt in 1420 although it has not always been an inn. During the late 18th and early 19th centuries it was divided into small dwellings and even did a stint as a workhouse. It was not until around 1900 that it opened as a hotel.

The Mermaid is full of atmosphere – old beams and hanging ivy, bedroom floors that slope, small casement windows, stairs with treads of different heights, vast fireplaces, murals here and there, and a tiny courtyard with a fountain playing. Over the years various visitors have asserted the inn is haunted. Dorothy, who worked there for some years, has had several people relate their experiences to her and what is more interesting is that the happenings took place in different bedrooms.

A guest staying in bedroom 1 woke up in the night and plainly saw a figure in white sitting on a chair in the corner. A lady who passed the night in bedroom 19 said there was something moving about on her bed. In fact, she made her two grown sons, who were sharing an adjacent bedroom, drag their mattresses into her room so that she would not be on her own. Then there was the man in bedroom 5 or 6 who asked if it were possible that a member of staff had walked through his bedroom in the night. When assured that this could not happen, he said, 'Well, I definitely saw someone walking across the room.'

Mermaid Inn, Rye. There appears to be the head of a ghostly man at the bottom of the small window on the top right-hand side.

In March 1962 my brother and his wife spent their honeymoon at the Mermaid. Like many other romantic couples, they booked the Elizabethan Chamber with its magnificent four-poster bed. They locked the door and retired to bed but were somewhat disconcerted when in the middle of the night the door swung open by itself.

In 1991 my daughter took the photograph of the Mermaid appearing in this book. When the film came back from the printers we were surprised to see what seemed to be the head of a man with beard and moustache. If you look closely at the bottom of the small window at the top right-hand side, perhaps you can see it too. Other people say it is nothing more than trick of light. But it is interesting all the same.

* * *

Also situated in Mermaid Street is Jeake's House, where the foundation stone was laid precisely at noon on 13th June 1689. Samuel Jeake was a student of astrology and the horoscope he cast for this building was by nature of an experiment. But he must have got it right because it has survived and flourished. He also cast a horoscope when it came to the important business of choosing a bride. And well he might, seeing as his intended was only twelve years old. They married on 1st March 1681 when she was thirteen but their first child was not born until three years later.

Jeake's House, Rye.

The house was originally built as a wool store; in 1853 the Baptists converted it into a school and in 1909 it became a dwelling house. Conrad Aiken (1889–1973), the American author and poet, purchased Jeake's House in 1924 and occupied the property for 23 years. In 1928 he bought the neighbouring property – by then a men's club but once a Baptist chapel. During his residence there he had many notable visitors, including Radclyffe Hall, E.F. Benson and T.S. Eliot. Aiken wrote about his home: 'by how many noble or beautiful or delightful spirits had it been lighted and blessed.' Presumably he was referring to his friends, but perhaps it was also an oblique reference to ghosts.

Jeake's House was partially derelict by the 1980s when Jenny Hadfield and her husband decided to restore it and open a guesthouse. They also acquired the house next door where once the Elders of the church had lived.

One resident ghost, known as the Blue Lady, appears to move between Jeake's House and the house opposite. Jenny describes the ghost as friendly and peaceful although they have never met. But three people who have seen her gave a similar description. In the 1980s a 14-year-old girl living opposite saw the Blue Lady at an upstairs window at Jeake's. She also noticed some people entering the room, completely oblivious to the ghost's presence. Jenny's uncle knew there was a ghost in that room and saw her too. The third sighting was by a chambermaid who caught sight of a figure clad in blue out of the corner of her eye. But when she turned her head to have a proper look, there was nobody there.

In August 2004 Jenny told me the ghosts are still active and this despite the fact that the lady in the house opposite had summoned the vicar to perform an exorcism in the 1990s.

The Blue Lady has been seen most often in the Four-poster Suite but there has also been a sighting of a female ghost in similar attire although not of the colour blue. Strange experiences have occurred in other rooms too – sheets tweaked by an invisible hand, bedside lamps levitating from table to pillow and the sound of footsteps overhead in an empty room. On one occasion a male guest felt a hand placed firmly on his shoulder. Thinking it was his wife, he turned round and saw a shadow, but his wife was fast asleep in bed.

A man wearing a tri-cornered hat has been spotted sitting at the bar and a mirror once fell off the wall although the picture hook remained in place, and in the parlour a large wall-mounted plate fell down for no apparent reason. Perhaps the most mysterious happening occurred in early June 2004 when there were three loud raps on the wall at 3.30 am, followed by the collapse of a round, glass-topped table – the glass being completely shattered.

It is interesting to note that a psychic found the atmosphere of Jeake's House somewhat overwhelming and stated in a weary voice that he really did not want to see anything more. When Jenny replied that she had never had even one glimpse of a ghost, he replied enigmatically, 'They don't need to show themselves to you, of course!'

SEAFORD

Some years ago Mrs Brankin, an elderly lady, lived in Seaford, looked after by her daughter Adrienne. One Sunday afternoon Adrienne decided to go to church with her friend as there seemed no danger in leaving her mother alone for a short time – her condition being quite stable. They went to St Leonard's, the old parish church of Seaford.

Sitting in the pew, listening to the sermon with half an ear, Adrienne began to glance around at other members of the congregation. She felt drawn to looking over her shoulder, hoping that the vicar would not notice her inattention. To her surprise she saw Mrs Brankin sitting in another pew, looking quite serene and composed. Shocked, she nudged her friend, who turned and recognised the figure too. This looked solid enough but they both knew that the old lady was bedridden and quite incapable of walking that far.

When the congregation rose to their feet at the end of the sermon, they took another look and saw that the pew was empty. They hurried home and found that Mrs Brankin had died at the precise moment they had seen her sitting quietly in St Leonard's church.

* * *

The Old Plough pub in Church Street used to be haunted. There were the usual manifestations such as glasses being moved around in the bar, objects shifted about in the cellar, and the odd noise and bump. A little more unusual was the cigarette smoke observed curling upwards, and you could smell it too. In the 1970s the landlords, Roger and Pearl Weston, did some research and found out that a White Russian by the name of Zilda had lived and died in the house. Moreover she had been a heavy smoker. At length the atmosphere became so spooky that staff refused to go in the cellar, while the hair on the back of the landlord's alsatian dog used to stand on end. The Westons asked the vicar for his assistance and after the house was blessed, the haunting ceased.

WEST BLATCHINGTON

On 21st April 1934 a report in the *Brighton Herald* stated that a shepherd employed by farmer Arthur Paul had been 'on three separate occasions the unwilling spectator of a nerve-shattering ghostly apparition.' The shepherd lived in a cottage near St Peter's church but as it was the lambing season, he was tending his sheep and young lambs in an old barn between

West Blatchington with windmill and barns,
and the top of St Helen's church visible in the background.

midnight and 1 am for a few nights before Easter that year. He was accompanied by his trusty collie sheepdog, and he carried a storm lantern. On the first occasion, soon after the shepherd entered the barn, his lantern went out. 'Then followed a rattling of the doors and shutters, and from the large window at the end of the building came a bright light and the white-clad form of a woman appeared. The apparition floated along the wall on one side of the barn, the whole distance, vanishing through a door at the opposite end into a dark room.' The shepherd was unable to light his lantern until he was outside the barn. Meanwhile the collie barked furiously while the sheep, which had glanced up as the figure glided past, huddled together and shrank backwards. There was exactly the same procedure on the second night but the third and fourth nights were uneventful. However, on the fifth night the whole weird spectacle was repeated. This was quite enough for the shepherd and, very shaken by his experiences, he refused to enter the barn at night again. Mr Paul had a new shed constructed elsewhere in which the sheep and newborn lambs could be tended as necessary.

WESTHAM

I t is thought that the church, which is dedicated to St Mary and is of Norman origin, once served the community of the Hospital of St Cross situated outside the west gate of Pevensey Castle. But the ghost haunting the churchyard is not an ancient shade but a more recent spirit who appears clad in a smart suit. Perhaps suits are not standard dress today but in October 1978 when Michael Stone saw the figure, it looked so ordinary that he smiled and wished it 'Good afternoon'. It was only when he opened the churchyard gate and the man vanished that he realised he had seen a ghost. This was not a one-off situation either because in October 1995 Charles Brownlow had a similar experience.

St Mary's church, Westham.

WESTMESTON

Not far from Ditchling Beacon is the village of Westmeston, which is haunted, it is said, by a large black dog. There is a nasty peculiarity about this animal – it is headless. The story goes that the black dog was once the pride of a local family. It had a wild streak and strangers approached it at their peril. Then the dog began to chase game. His owners were warned but dismissed it as malicious gossip. When the gamekeeper found a young deer savaged to death, he had a good idea of the culprit. He began to take his blunderbuss out with him on his rounds and it was only a matter of time before he saw the dog chasing a deer. He had no hesitation in firing off his gun. He killed the dog all right but the blunderbuss is a not a selective instrument and the blast blew off the dog's head.

* * *

Westmeston Place was once haunted by the ghost of a monk, killed during the Reformation. It seems he was busy carving a panel when his attackers burst in.

People who have seen the ghost always mention the half-finished carving in the background. It was a good tale and people loved to recount it. But eventually the owners grew weary of it and in 1925 had the panel removed and placed in Streat church where it forms part of the reredos. It seems to have done the trick and the ghost has not been seen at Westmeston Place since.

WINCHELSEA

There were two communities of friars in Winchelsea. The first to arrive were the Grey Friars (Franciscans) in the 1230s, followed by the Black Friars (Dominicans). Even when the sea overwhelmed much of Old Winchelsea during dreadful storms in 1250 and 1287, the Grey Friars and Black Friars built fresh establishments in New Winchelsea.

During the Dissolution of the Monasteries in the 16th century the friars were ejected and most buildings demolished but some chapels survived for the use of the local populace. At Winchelsea there are no visible traces of the Black Friars' house, but the chapel belonging to the Grey Friars and dedicated to the Virgin Mary has survived as a ruin. It is situated east of the house called, appropriately enough, Grey Friars. In the 1890s a Major Stileman lived in the house and kept a pet eagle on a chain in the chapel ruins.

It seems that one friar is reluctant to leave the scene of his former abode. Mr and Mrs Cook lived in a house called Cleveland Place in Friars Road. One Christmas Eve in the 1890s Mr Cook was walking home from the New Inn across the churchyard to Friars Road. As he approached the church porch he noticed a hazy light and stopped to look more closely. He was amazed when he saw the figure of a Grey Friar holding a lantern in his hand glide out of the shadows. Mr Cook watched the ghost turn left to go down Friars Road and he

St Thomas's church, Winchelsea.

followed. When he reached his front door, he paused and saw the ghost pass silently on to Grey Friars.

WIVELSFIELD

More House stands near the church and although part of it dates back to the 16th century, the tile-hung front is Georgian. The More family who owned the house favoured military careers and it is possible that, during a foray abroad, one of them acquired a Chinese servant who travelled back with them to Sussex. Such an exotic servant was seen as a sign of prestige but unfortunately the story goes that his master treated him harshly. It is a wonder that his ghost is not a malevolent shade, but according to Mrs Roger Hales who once lived in the house, they found him friendly. She said in 1978, 'I saw him on numerous occasions and he did me no harm.'

* * *

Despite its impressive title, Great Ote Hall is not huge but it is very interesting, with timber-framing, tall chimneys and a date-stone inscribed '1600'. In the 18th century Selina, Countess of Huntingdon lived in the house. She was a famous convert to Methodism and her chaplain was the Revd George Whitefield, a celebrated preacher of his day. In 1761 she built a chapel in the grounds of her house in North Street, Brighton, and in 1778 she built Ote Hall Chapel. So many people flocked to the Brighton chapel that she was obliged to enlarge the premises, financed by the sale of her jewellery for £700. She was responsible for the erection of a number of chapels, which went by the title of the Countess of Huntingdon's Connexion, and by the time she died in 1791 there were 64 of them. A great tragedy in her life was the death of her two sons from smallpox. Great Ote Hall is said to be haunted by a ghost and it is claimed it might be Selina.

* * *

Antye is a farmhouse dating from late Tudor times where the ghost of a little girl wearing a frilly white nightdress used to glide down the stairs. The writer Vida Herbison lived in the house as a youngster and recalled that her family called the ghost 'Annie'. Outside, the ghost of a carter from Regency times was sometimes spotted near the well seated on a low wall. It was especially odd because when the carter made an appearance the dogs would go and sit beside him. Usually animals do not like to go anywhere near a ghost.

* * *

Jacob Harris was a Jewish pedlar who had Anglicised his name from Hirsch and who travelled about the Sussex countryside in the 18th century. In May 1734 Harris lodged at the Royal Oak, Wivelsfield, situated on the northern edge of Ditchling Common. On the evening of 25th May he was interested to hear the landlord, Richard Miles, boast of his takings. The next day, Harris walked up to the landlord as he was seeing to the horses in the stables and cut his throat. A young serving girl, hearing the commotion, came downstairs to see what was going on and Harris killed her. Then he went upstairs to find the landlord's wife Dorothy, who was ill in bed, and he murdered her too. Miles did not die immediately but lingered on until 30th May and thus was able to name his assailant.

Retribution was swift – Harris was captured at the Cat inn, West Hoathly, tried, found guilty, and hanged at Horsham Gaol on 31st August 1734. His body was brought back to the scene of his crime and hung from chains on a gibbet set up on Ditchling Common as a horrific warning to passers-by. Local people perpetuated his memory by later erecting a post on the site of the gibbet surmounted by a rooster with the date '1734' cut into its metal body. Superstitious folk believed there was powerful magic in objects associated with a hanged man and Jacob's Post was chipped away piece by piece by those in search of a medical cure-all. The post had to be replaced – no doubt several times. People believed the site was haunted and gave the place a wide berth at night.

In May 1995 it was reported that there were spooky happenings at recently opened Ditchling Museum. The actor Donald Sinden recorded the story behind the triple killing on a tape. On Sunday, 26th May 1985 the tape went wrong and played back to front. It was only later that staff realised that the day was the 251st anniversary of the crime.

· Bibliography ·

Armstrong, J.R. *History of Sussex* (1961 reprinted 1978)

Bartley, L.J. *The Story of Bexhill*

Chapman, Brigid *East Sussex Inns* (1988)

Chapman, Brigid *West Sussex Inns* (1988)

Cheal, Henry *History of Ditchling* (1901, reprinted 2004)

Coxe, Antony D. Hippisley *Haunted Britain* (1973)

d'Enno, Douglas *Foul Deeds and Suspicious Deaths around Brighton* (2004)

Doyle, Sir Arthur *Memories and Adventures* (1924, paperback edition 1989)

Egerton, Revd John Coker *Sussex Folk and Sussex Ways* (1892)

Elvins, M.T. *Arundel Priory* (1981)

Erredge, H.E. *History of Bramber Castle*

Ford, Harry *Steyning Conservation Area Guide* (1980, revised 2003)

Forman, Joan *The Haunted South* (1978)

Fox-Wilson, Frank *The Story of Goring and Highdown* (1987)

Geering, Thomas *Our Sussex Parish* (1925, reprinted 2003)

Gilmour, David *The Long Recessional* (2002)

Green, Andrew *Haunted Sussex Today* (1997)

Gundry, Doris *Midhurst, Yesterday and Today* (1984)

Guy, John *Castles in Sussex* (1984)

Hall, Doris M. *A Stroll around Ditchling* (1987)

Hopkins, R. Thurston *Ghosts over England* (1953)

Hopkins, R. Thurston *The Lure of Sussex* (1928)

Ivett, Ivan *Steyning Conversations* (2002)

Jones, Kelvin I. *Conan Doyle and the Spirits* (1989)

Lewis, Harley *Theatre Ghosts* (1988)

Rackham, John *Brighton Ghosts, Hove Hauntings* (2001)

Scarry, S.J. *Horsham's Hidden Horrors* (1996)

Smith, Bernard & Haas, Peter *Writers in Sussex* (1985)

McEwan, Graham J. *Haunted Churches of England* (1989)

Moore, R. *Sussex Ghosts* (1976)

Norman, Mike *A Walkabout Guide to Shoreham*

Ray, David *Cowdray Ruins*

Surtees, John *Beachy Head* (1997)

Tales of Old Petworth (1976, reprinted 1987)

Taylor, Rupert *East Sussex Village Book* (1986)

● Bibliography ●

Taylor, Rupert *Murders of Old Sussex* (1991)
Trotter, Torrens *Cowdray Ruins* (1922, revised 1975)
Underwood, Peter *This Haunted Isle* (1984)
Wales, Tony *Sussex Customs, Curiosities and Country Lore* (1990)
Wales, Tony *Sussex Ghosts and Legends* (1992)
Wales, Tony *West Sussex Village Book* (1984)
Walkerley, Rodney L. *Sussex Pubs* (1966)

Various editions of the following periodicals:
Advertiser (West Sussex County Times Ltd), *Argus* formerly the *Evening Argus*, *Bexhill-on-Sea Observer*, *Bognor Guardian*, *Brighton Herald*, *Brighton & Hove Gazette & Herald*, *Brighton & Hove Leader*, *Sunday Telegraph*, *Sussex Express*, *Sussex County Magazine*, *Sussex Life*, *TV Times*, *West Sussex Gazette*

Acknowledgements

The author would like to thank the following people for their help: Mr V Landymore; Lilian Rogers; Mrs Mo Salmon; Michael Sullivan and Lynne Mason; Stephen Neiman of the Old Market, Hove; Shirley Brennan of the Chichester pub in Chichester; Sue Gilson of the *Chichester Observer*; Jenny Hadfield of Jéake's House, Rye; Robert Jeeves of Step Back in Time, Brighton; Peter Jerome of Petworth; Mark Nelson of First Light, Brighton; Chris Tod of Steyning Museum; the staff of the Mermaid Inn, Rye, and of Ockenden Manor, Cuckfield; the reference staff of Worthing and Horsham Libraries. Thanks are also due to all those people who shared their stories with me.

Illustrations

The illustrations are from photographs taken by the author or old postcards in the author's collection unless otherwise stated.

· Index ·